THE RIVER THAMES

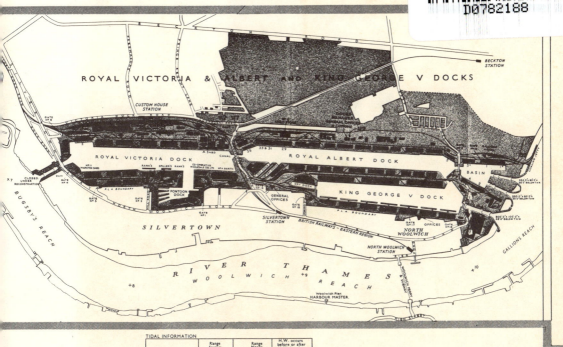

TIDAL INFORMATION	Range Springs FEET	Range Neaps FEET	H.W. occurs before or after H.W. London HR. MIN
Richmond	7.85	3.85	1.01 after
Hammersmith	17.40	13.00	.38 after
London Bridge	21.67	14.99	ZERO
Royal Albert Dock	21.39	14.54	.21 before
Tilbury	19.29	12.87	.52 before
Southend	17.11	11.20	1.17 before

P.L.A. TIDE GAUGES SHOWN 5

1 Richmond ... Recording Tide Gauge
2 Tower Pier ... ...
3 North Woolwich Pier ... ...
4 Purfleet ... Illuminated Tide Gauge
★5 Tilbury ... Recording & Illuminated Tide Gauge
★6 Southend ... Recording Tide Gauge
★7 Shivering Sands Tower ... Recording Tide Gauge & Daylight Tide Board
★8 Margate ... Recording Tide Gauge
★9 Walton-on-the-Naze ...

★The height of tide at these places is repeated by radio link to the Thames Navigation Service—Gravesend.

STORM SIGNALS
Tilbury — Southend Pier
DISTANCES
Distances above or below London Bridge are shown in land miles thus: 5

Scale of Feet
5000 10000 15000 20000 25000 30000

Scale of Kilometres
1 0 1 2 3 4 5 6 7 8 9 10

THE PORT OF LONDON

THE PORT OF LONDON

by

R. DOUGLAS BROWN

TERENCE DALTON LIMITED
LAVENHAM . SUFFOLK
1978

Published by
TERENCE DALTON LIMITED

ISBN 0 900963 87 5

Text photoset in 11/12pt. Baskerville

Printed in Great Britain at
THE LAVENHAM PRESS LIMITED
LAVENHAM   .   SUFFOLK

Contents

Index of Illustrations

TO ELSIE

My beloved Londoner

Introduction and Acknowledgement

THERE is no other port in the world which has so influenced the patterns of international trade over so long a period of history as the Port of London. The Romans built its first quays. The merchants of all medieval Europe met on London Bridge. The Elizabethan merchant-adventurers sailed from the Thames to open up new continents. The system of enclosed docks constructed in the nineteenth century symbolised the energy and inventiveness of the British nation in the epoch of imperialism. And, in the twentieth century, the Port of London was among the first major industrial undertakings to confront the economic, political and social problems thrown up by the pace of technological innovation.

Any story so rich in colour and drama must, as events unfold, be constantly told and retold. We can read of the Port of London in the histories of Tacitus and Bede, in the poetry of Chaucer and Shakespeare, and in a whole library of books of more recent times. Why, then, another?

At a time when the very survival of London as a port is seriously challenged, it is appropriate to reassess past achievements, present performance and future prospects. Today we can understand, as perhaps never before, that the port is a microcosm of Britain. Throughout history, it has faithfully mirrored the fortunes of the nation. Here we may discern evidence of the state of national morale, measure the current standard of performance of the British people, assess the standing and relative economic strength of Britain in the international community. Here we may study the impact of new technology and the tensions which it creates as the drive for efficiency and competitive pricing sometimes comes into apparent conflict with the fundamental human aspiration to work satisfaction and economic security. Viewed against the new perspectives, London's glow of pride in its port belongs to the past—and, one hopes, to the future. But, for the present, the wind up the river strikes chill.

In the pages that follow I have endeavoured to avoid argument and to let the facts speak for themselves. I recognise, however, that the selection and presentation of facts involves a subjective presentation, and for this I am entirely responsible.

I should like to acknowledge with gratitude the assistance I have received in gathering facts and photographs from many members, or former members, of the staff of the Port of London Authority, but particularly from Mr Geoffrey Morgan, Mr Graham Avory and Mr Dick Brown. I am grateful, too, to the staffs of museums and picture libraries acknowledged in the captions, and to Mr Peter Coppock, for assistance in selecting suitable illustrations—

particularly to the staff of the Photographic Department of the Museum of London, into whose care the P.L.A. has passed the collection of photographs which it built up over the first half of the present century.

I wish to thank Dick Fagan and Eric Burgess, the authors, and Robert Hale Ltd, the publishers, for permission to quote from *Men of the Tideway*, and the executors of G. D. H. Cole and Raymond Postgate and their publishers, Methuen & Co Ltd, for permission to quote from *The Common People, 1746-1938*.

R. DOUGLAS BROWN

Stoke-by-Clare, Suffolk.
August 1978.

The Classic Clippers. These were arguably the most beautiful trading vessels ever built. They sailed regularly to the Thames in the nineteenth century, bringing tea from the Orient and wool and grain from Australia. This coloured lithograph by T. G. Dutton, published in 1866, shows the tea clippers *Ariel* and *Taeping*.   *Courtesy Trustees of the National Maritime Museum*

CHAPTER ONE

The Thames Tideway

THE first boat which sailed the Thames Tideway faced a daunting task of
exploration. No-one knows who those sailors were, nor when they made
their voyage, but it must have been a very long time before the Romans came
or our written history began. With an effort of imagination, however, we can
savour something of their experience. They came from the land across the
Channel, which was Gaul. They sailed in a small, wooden tub of a boat,
propelled and steered by oars, with a single square sail to help when the wind
was right. Their first rule of navigation was to remain always within sight of
coast. Our imaginary voyage began then, in all probability, on a clear summer
day when the coast of south-eastern England would be seen from across the
Channel, a beckoning challenge to an adventurous spirit. Picking up the white
chalk of South Foreland, the little boat turned north. The cliffs fell back and
there was an open marshland estuary, but the temptation to explore there was
resisted. Ahead the chalk cliffs of the North Foreland presented a new
challenge. What lay around the corner?

The answer was the Thames Estuary, but those first sailor explorers would
not have known for some time that they were heading into a river. They could
see land only on their port, and that was an endless panorama of sand and
mud and marsh, with a vast dome of sky above. All around broad banks of
sand broke the surface, frayed by innumerable channels. There was a maze of
creeks among the sedge and reeds and rushes. Waterfowl bobbed and splashed
there and wild swans screeched and beat their wings overhead.

Wherever the water lay still and clear, the fish swam in shoals, with
salmon and trout in plenty. As the sun crossed a blue sky, this was an
attractive, exhilarating scene; but when dusk fell, mists drifted about the
marshes and a quiet melancholy settled down with the night.

With dawn, our explorers pressed on. They must have sailed, by chance,
to the north of what was (though they did not know it) a marshy island one day
to be known as Sheppey, and past the mouth of a river which now we know as
Medway. Their course was then set for the discovery of the Thames. They saw
mainland on either beam. In the clear light of morning the distant wooded
hills of Kent rose beyond the marshes, while northward, across an estuary eight
miles wide, they could discern a gently rolling landscape green-brown with
scrub and trees, with a line of low hills beyond.

1

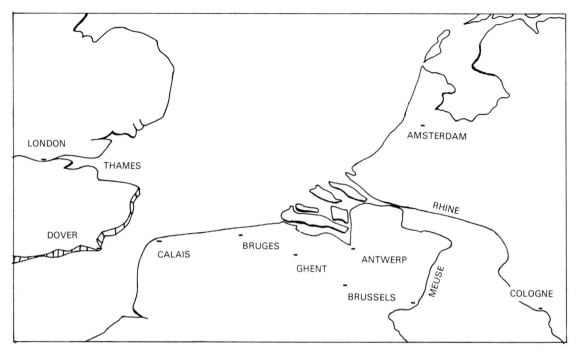

The Thames estuary lies opposite the mouths of the rivers Rhine, Maas and Waal, which flow into Germany, Switzerland, Belgium and France. This geographical alignment has been of great significance throughout almost two thousand years of maritime and mercantile history.

Now the sailors were carried forward by a tide which ran for five or six hours at a steady two or three miles each hour. When it turned, they were still not very far from the open sea, so they must have landed or anchored, and waited for the succeeding tide. When their voyage resumed, the river channel narrowed a little and followed enormous sweeping curves, so that sometimes their boat was sailing almost due north or due south as its generally-westward progress was maintained. After sailing for forty miles from the North Foreland, the river was still two miles across and there was nothing to see but water and sky and wild marsh vegetation. Where one day Gravesend and Tilbury would arise, there was complete solitude for these first explorers, but as they covered the succeeding twenty miles of curving river their keen eyes began to observe important changes in the landscape. To the south, high land approached the river more closely and eventually reached the water's edge as a low bluff with a gravel strand below it. There may have been a small Celtic settlement (near the site of present-day Gravesend); if so, it was probably the first sight of other human beings they had had since entering the estuary. This bluff was the first of several on the south bank observed as the ship sailed on; the chalk cliff bordering the flood plain touches the river at half-a-dozen places and at each there could well have been a small settlement — precursors of towns today called Northfleet, Greenhithe, Erith, Woolwich and Greenwich. On the northern side of the river a number of streams flowed into wide, marshy creeks; the first travellers had no names for them, but we know them as the Mar Dyke at Purfleet, the Ingrebourne River running into Rainham Creek, the Beam River at Dagenham, the River Roding feeding into Barking Creek, and the River Lea. The estuary of the Lea was once a mile wide, so that to the first Thames sailors it presented a wide vista of open water. On the south side of the river, Dartford Creek received what is now the Darent River and Deptford Creek the Ravensbourne.

Once past the Lea, an immense area of marshland lay directly ahead. The main Thames channel doubled back on itself, actually flowed south-south-east for more than a mile, looped the marshes, washed over sandbanks which at low tide almost blocked the channel completely, and then opened out into a large pool beneath a hill. There, for practical purposes, the tide ran out. Our travellers had arrived. This was to become the Pool of London.

Nature provided the tides, the pool and the hill, and in conjunction these decided the site upon which the Port of London was to rise. For centuries the tides dictated all shipping movements in the river, providing the motive power which brought ships to their berths. The Pool gave the area and depth of water in which they could manoeuvre and tie up. The hill provided a good base on land, with a satisfactory water supply, and vegetation, game and fish for food. Two streams flowed into the Pool, one of them making a notch in the contours of the hill, the other at its western foot; each was only a few miles long, but 25 to 30 feet wide at the mouth. One day they would be known as the Fleet and the Wallbrook.

Across the main stream from the hill a broad spur of dry gravel came through the surrounding marshes and this was the first point in the whole stretch of tidal water which lent itself to a crossing by ferry. Lower down, there had been the bluffs on the southern bank, but no firm foothold on the northern. Here, for the first time, there was firm, dry land within half a mile of the river on both sides, which could not be inundated at high tides. Beyond the eastern slope of the hill, marshes stretched away for about three miles as far as the Lea river. Northward, there were more hills and varied vegetation: alder, willow, oak, birch, chestnut and hazel. It was a healthy site, with basic resources at hand, and lending itself to effective defence. Probably the new arrivals found a settlement of Celts in possession, living in wattle and daub huts on the slopes above the river. Possibly they met them first on the water; the London Museum holds among the earliest relics found in the area an oak plank, tapered at each end, and a hollowed oak trunk and these, along with the coracle, were the first craft used by local inhabitants.

We can only guess at the nature of that first encounter, and the many others that must have followed; there is virtually no historical evidence.

The Thames flows in a series of great bends through East London on its way to the sea. The old London Docks can be seen at the bottom of the photograph, centre, and the Old Surrey Commercial Docks above them, to the right. The West India and Millwall Docks can be seen on the Isle of Dogs, within the great horseshoe bend of the river, and beyond them the three Royal Docks. Tilbury Docks lie at the most distant point on the river visible in this picture.

Aerofilms Limited

Though Celtic Britain traded with the Continent, exporting slaves, hides, tin and lead, it is unlikely that any cargoes passed along the Thames. When Julius Caesar, planning his first invasion of Britain, cross-examined merchants in Gaul, their knowledge does not seem to have extended beyond the sea-coast immediately across the Channel. When Caesar landed here in 54 B.C. and advanced to the old British citadel at Verulam (St Albans), he crossed the Thames up-stream of the Pool and his description of the expedition makes no reference to any settlement on the site of London. By 61 A.D., however, on the authority of the Roman historian Tacitus (whose father-in-law was Roman Governor of Britain for a time), London had become an important centre for businessmen and their merchandise, though still falling short of the status of a Roman settlement.

It is a reasonable deduction that once Caesar had opened the road from Rome to Verulam, traders came hard upon his heels, and that contacts between Britain and the Roman empire in Gaul were on a regular basis. Cymbeline (or Cunobelin), ruler of half-a-dozen Belgic tribes in southern England during the first forty years A.D., seems to have encouraged this trade, and indeed all things Roman. When he died, the Emperor Claudius resolved upon the incorporation of Britain into the Empire and in 44 A.D. it was effectively occupied by Vespasian.

London's earliest growth as a trading centre may have owed less to its river position than to its situation between the British cities of Verulam and Camulodunum (Colchester) to the north and the Channel ports which provided a short sea crossing to the Continent. For some time after their arrival, the Romans used the overland route through Kent from Portus Dubris (Dover) to Verulam, fording the Thames on the way. Despite new Roman roads, however, water offered an easier means of transporting goods. The River Lea flowed within a dozen miles of Verulam and gave direct access to the Thames, which could then be safely used as far as Gravesend. Below that the esturarial waters presented dangers, which were avoided by arranging overland porterage across northern Kent to a new port, Rutupiae (Richborough), which the Romans built, probably in the third century, on the east coast of Kent.

The Romans, with their capacity for accurate survey, must have quickly appreciated the potential of London as a commercial centre and port. The geographical and geological character of the Thames valley was significant; a great V-shaped funnel between chalk outcrops, the Chilterns to the north and the North Downs to the south, with the river flowing through it after breaking through the chalk wall below Goring. The mouth of the funnel directly faced North-Eastern Gaul, provinces of the Roman empire which had developed a vigorous trading tradition centred upon Flanders, with the Maas and the Rhine rivers serving as highways to the interior of the continent and beyond. London was the classic bridge-port at the head of an estuary, and this particular estuary opened out on to a continental land-mass which represented the whole of the known world.

We may speculate that the Romans concentrated upon the development of the river and the port. The navigational problems of the outer estuary would have been solved, so that vessels bound to and from London could complete their voyages without trans-shipment. Roman engineers doubtless deepened the channels where it was necessary. There is no evidence, however, that they embanked the river in any systematic way; and it was embankment which first controlled the Thames tideway so that it served the port efficiently. When, in due time, both sides of the channel were embanked from the Pool to Gravesend, 42½ square miles of marshland were reclaimed; a sluggish stream was converted into a fast-running one, perhaps doubling the speed of the tide and extending the period of its useful motive power. By confining the river to something like one tenth of its previous area, the channels were scoured and deepened.

So who embanked, and when? Reasonably, we may guess that some of the work was carried out over a very long period in Saxon, Danish and Norman times, to protect various riverside settlements as they sprang up down-stream. Sir Joseph Broodbank, in his *History of the Port of London*, chose a theory that most of the work was completed by Flemish immigrants—with much experience of land reclamation in their own country—who came to England in the wake of William of Normandy. He drew attention to the fact that the earliest statutes of which we have copies relate to embankment during Henry III's reign (1216-1272), but refer back to laws passed by his grandfather Henry II (1154-1189). This would make the construction of the embankments almost contemporaneous with the construction of the first permanent stone bridge across the river—the London Bridge of history and legend which stood for over six centuries before it was replaced.

Once embanked, no significant changes in the river occurred over many centuries. Not until the beginning of the nineteenth century could the river bed be scientifically charted and the main channel accurately defined. At that time, and for many years afterwards, there was a 24 feet channel as far as Erith, but in Barking and Woolwich Reaches there were depths of less than 12 feet at low tide. Under very favourable conditions vessels drawing up to 18 feet might make the whole journey from Gravesend to the Pool on one tide; more usually, there was waiting between tides in Long Reach or at Erith, Woolwich or Blackwall. The larger vessels, including the East Indiamen, could never get beyond Blackwall or Deptford.

It was not until the present century, with the formation of the Port of London Authority, that a systematic, large-scale enlargement of the channel took place. Earlier efforts had produced 18 feet of depth as far as the Royal Docks entrance in Galleons Reach. Now the longest deep-water channel in the world was created by dredging over 50 million tons of soil. A broad, graded channel, with smoothed curves, provided over 27 feet of water at low tide as far as the entrance to the Royal Docks and over 20 feet to all other docks except the London and St Katharine. Taking tide into account, this meant that there was over 34 feet of water for more than five hours on every tide of the year as far up as the King George V Dock. The work continued over twenty-five years; when it was completed, vessels of 20,000 tons were able regularly to reach the Royals and in 1939 the 35,655-ton Cunard liner *Mauretania* sailed up the Thames and berthed in the King George V Dock. Its appearance there symbolised the ultimate development of the Thames Tideway.

A line engraving of troops crossing from Gravesend to Tilbury Fort in 1780. This shows vessels with ramps, early ancestors of the modern landing craft.

This conjectural bird's-eye view of the walled city of London in Roman times, showing quays below a wooden bridge across the Thames, was drawn by A. Forestier.

CHAPTER TWO

The River Port

BECAUSE London has taken its place in history as the great *world* port, its evolution and progress cannot be explained or understood without some description of the world of which it has been part. Its citizens may well claim special virtues which have contributed to their fame and fortune, but they must not press the claim too far, for immigration over the centuries has introduced many different racial influences upon the Cockney character. Indeed, it can be shown that at several stages in the city's history its native residents were slow to grasp the opportunities which arose. The fact that Britain was an island at first emphasized its position at the outer rim of the known world and may have deterred it from precipitate involvement; later this geographical isolation enabled it to become the vantage point, the focus field and the natural meeting place of those whose view was European and, later, world-wide.

As we begin our survey of the city and the port, it is an outpost of empire, but not an unimportant one. Much new evidence about the shape of Roman London has been unearthed in recent times. In the summer of 1977 Post Office engineers, driving a 100-feet-long telephone cable tunnel under the City, bisected the site of the Roman Forum and so we now know that this was 500 feet long, that it stood where Gracechurch Street exists today, that it was the heart of the Roman City, and the administrative and judicial centre. Shops and stalls, under porticoes, lined three of its sides, and an immense basilica stood along the other. Between this forum and the Thames, running parallel with the river, was a principal thoroughfare where all commercial activity was concentrated, with side roads giving access to the water-front. Throughout history that thoroughfare has been called, as it remains today, Thames Street. The whole of the Roman City was encircled by a great wall, raised in the third century, which was 20 feet high and eight feet thick at its base. It ran for three miles to enclose an area of 330 acres, from the river at what is now Blackfriars, along the line of the Fleet river to Ludgate, and thence to Newgate, Aldersgate, Cripplegate, Bishopsgate and Aldgate back to the river at the point where the Tower of London was later to be raised. The whole of the river front was walled, too, but there were water-gates which gave access to two Roman quays: one at Billingsgate and the other at Dowgate, at the mouth of the Wallbrook (where Cannon Street railway station now stands). There may have been, but it is surmise, another gate giving access to a timber bridge across the river to the south bank.

Roman barges were of impressive size, as may be seen by visitors to the London Museum, where one found at Blackfriars has been carefully reconstructed in cross-section. It is recorded that by 359 Britain was exporting 800 cargoes of corn each year to store-houses on the Rhine; it is likely that most of it passed through London, either by river or by road. In earliest Roman times most shipments probably went down the Thames only as far as the present site of Gravesend, and were there taken on by road to Richborough for re-shipment across the channel. The hazards of the outer Thames Estuary were only gradually overcome, and then of dire necessity; by the end of the third century the Saxons had begun to attack the east coast and in 296 an enemy fleet sailed up the Thames, broke into London, and there was bitter fighting in the streets. The Romans appointed a "Count of the Saxon Shore" with a fleet and 10,000 men to protect the coast from Brancaster to Shoreham, and from then until the eventual Roman withdrawal from Britain, this defence force was constantly in action. All Thames waters must then have become very familiar, so that direct sea routes to the Rhine were secured.

The last Romans pulled out of England in 410 and the occupation by Saxons, Angles and Jutes which followed was part of a movement of northern tribes into the heart of Europe, establishing new kingdoms as they took over most of the Roman territory. Great migrations of population surged and ebbed across the continent as the old empires of Rome and Constantinople expanded and contracted, as the Northmen in increasing numbers crossed the North Sea and the Rhine and Danube rivers, as the armies of Islam pressed relentlessly from east and south, and Slav invaders made incursions from the north-east. Britain, throughout this period, lay at the furthest frontier, but what happened on the continent was of the greatest significance for its development as a port.

We know very little of Saxon London. The first nearby Saxon settlements were probably along the north bank of the Thames east of the City and a commercial relationship with Romano-Britons within the walls may well have grown up. By 604 Aethelbert, established as king of Kent, was in a position to instal the first bishop of London and a year later the Saxons were fully in control of the City. Aethelbert had married a Frankish princess, Bercta of Paris, who had been converted to Christianity and this opened the way for the arrival from Rome of Augustus, who was installed as Archbishop at Canterbury and thus became the founder of the English church. Here was a powerful combination. Aethelbert brought the country as far north as the Wash under his control. The church was also able to deploy considerable resources, if of a different kind. The Church of Rome, since its acceptance as the state religion, had grown rich and had attracted many men of special talent.

10

The alliance of Church and Court in England closely parallelled a similar trend throughout Europe. When Charlemagne had driven the frontiers of his realm into northern Spain, into Italy, Austria, north-eastern Germany and Scandinavia, Pope Leo III was ready, in the year 800, to place a crown upon his head and proclaim him the first head of the Holy Roman Empire. The whole balance of the medieval world had swung from the Mediterranean to the North Sea. A new empire flourished, with a settled agricultural base and established centres of commerce at Bruges and Ghent, Antwerp and Cologne. And all these cities were in close trading association with London. There are no records of the trade of London in Saxon times, but Bede (673-735) recorded that the City was "the mart of many nations resorting to it by sea and land". The benefits were shared by Court and Church. The kings imposed direct taxes on all shipments. The great monasteries were middlemen between wool farmers and merchants, and wool was the basis of the nation's wealth.

The empire of Charlemagne did not hold together. From the north came new invaders, the Vikings. From 787 they constantly raided along the east coast of England and sailed on to harry the southern shore. London had its first taste of the new invaders in 851, when a fleet of 350 longboats came into the mouth of the Thames and disembarked a raiding force to attack London and Canterbury. The Vikings were back in 879, 886, and then at regular intervals throughout the tenth century. They occupied much of southern England but London, which became a cockpit of the struggle, held out against them until 1017, when it accepted Knud (Canute) as king. Meanwhile, other Viking forces swept into Paris and Rouen and Cologne; sailed east across the Baltic and found their way by river to Novgorod, the great trading centre of Russia; navigated by waterway to the Black Sea and so to Constantinople, and to the Caspian Sea and so to Baghdad, thus establishing links with the world of Islam and with the Orient; occupied Iceland and Greenland, and even reached America. In the end, they held all the coastlines of the Baltic, the North Sea and the coast of France as far south as the Garonne, and they established their great new trading centre in eastern Sweden. The Mediterranean's golden millenium ended, as a self-confident, thrusting northern culture imposed new patterns everywhere. Just across the Channel, in Flanders, large tracts of marshy coastland were reclaimed from the sea. Elsewhere, forests were cleared and more careful farming provided surplus produce for sale, for the first time. Market-places and roads, bridges and wharves were built. Workshops sprang up everywhere. Old habits of barter were swept away as the establishment of mints brought a new money-based economy. The new merchant class rapidly acquired wealth. The artisans multiplied and prospered. There was a rapid increase in population. Schools were established and architecture, art and literature flourished.

Before the Vikings triumphed, Saxon rulers of England had begun doing

London Bridge, about 1600. This nineteenth century lithograph reproduces a Visscher print first published in 1616. It shows the substantial buildings incorporated in the bridge. Above the southern gateway the heads of criminals are displayed on pikes.

their best to develop trading links with Europe. Aethelstain in 938 offered rewards to any London merchant who could organise three voyages to the continent and back. Edgar (958-975) admitted merchants from Cologne, Dortmund, Munster, Utrecht, Bremen and Hamburg to conduct business in London and this arrangement was formalised by Aethelred (979-1016), who extended the invitation to other associates of the German merchants who were developing trade along the Rhine and the Elbe. They came to settle in London and were greeted as Emperor's Men (because their homes were in the Holy Roman Empire) or as Easterlings. Their story, as we shall see, is one of the most remarkable in the whole history of the port.

The old Roman quays at Dowgate and Billingsgate still formed, at this period, the principal parts of the port, but there were probably some other berthing places; there are references to "Ludentune's hythe" in 734. The first informative document about the port dates from 990, in the last phase of Saxon rule, under Aethelred. He had married Emma, daughter of Duke Richard of Normandy, and one result was that vessels from Poitou, Normandy and France "showed their goods and went toll-free". The same document records the agreement with the Easterlings; they could trade in their own ships and market their goods freely in London, subject to payment of the ordinary tolls and to two special gifts, to be made at Easter and Christmas. On these occasions the king was to receive two bales of grey cloth and one of brown, ten pounds of pepper, five pairs of gloves and two casks of vinegar. Dues and tolls for other traffic were also set down. Boats calling at the wharf at Billingsgate were to pay one halfpenny, or a penny if they were with sail. If they berthed, the toll was fourpence. Fishing vessels were charged according to size: a halfpenny for small ones, a penny for larger ones. From each cargo of timber one log was taken as toll, from each basket of fowls one fowl, and from each basket of eggs five eggs. Vessels from Rouen with wine or dried fish paid six sous and five per cent of their fish cargo. The document makes it clear that there was a general market around the wharves where Londoners bought and sold. Women who came to this market to sell butter and cheese were required to pay a penny a fortnight before Christmas and a further penny a week later.

When Knud replaced the last of the Saxon kings, he was already king of Denmark. He married the widow of the old king, Aethelred, thus preserving the established trading links with Normandy, and so Britain was as closely integrated into Europe as ever she has been. One of the astonishing things about life in those remote times was the readiness with which kings, nobles, bishops and merchants travelled vast distances, repeatedly crossing the length and breadth of the continent. Even before Aethelred had taken **his** Norman bride, Otto the Great, crowned Emperor in Rome in 962, had taken an English one. And when his successor, Conrad II, was crowned in 1024 Knud travelled from England as a coronation guest. As a new medieval European society emerged, merchants went everywhere, regularly attending trade fairs in France, the Low Countries, Sweden and Italy. Goods were bought and sold and passed back to regional wholesalers who sold to local peddlers. The communications network, depending entirely on the spoken word, stretched into the most remote villages. Depots were required along the developing trade routes and thus new towns were built. In the year 1000 there were no towns in Europe with a population of 10,000; within one hundred years a new urban society had been created and among the towns with more than 20,000 population were Hamburg and Antwerp, Cologne and Bruges, Paris and Rouen, Venice and Genoa . . . and London.

London traded in every direction and with the traders who came to the Thames there came tales, not only of fact but of fable. The latter grew from the fleeting contacts in far places with traders of other races living beyond distant oceans. To give substance to their more colourful stories, the London traders brought home such things as had never been seen before: ivory and spices, jewellery and silken goods. Most of these had been obtained in Constantinople, whence they had been brought by camel caravan from

Bokhara and beyond, or by dhow by way of the Indian Ocean and the Red Sea from China, India and Ceylon.

By the second half of the eleventh century the Vikings had settled down in their new European territories, had accepted Christianity, intermarried with the local people, adopted local languages. Across the Channel, the northmen had become Normans, and their country Normandy. A nobleman there, who was only five generations removed from Rollo, the original Viking invader, set his eyes upon London, and planned an invasion of his own. William, Duke of Normandy, was crowned King of England on Christmas Day 1066 in a London which was already a large, impressive and prosperous capital city, seething with energy and expectation, even if not particularly pleasing to the eye. Many of the old Roman buildings were crumbling or ruined, even the great encircling wall, particularly along the water-front, where some of its masonry had probably been incorporated in new wharves and piers. Around these, and a great timber bridge over the river, a complex of warehouses had developed so that, for about a mile along the northern bank downstream from the mouth of the Fleet, a busy port was established. Tracks sloped down from Thames Street to piers built out over the tidal mud, at which single ships could berth. At two or three places the mud had probably been excavated and wooden piles sunk, so that rectangular basins capable of taking several vessels had been created. Between these and the surrounding warehouses, there would have been a constant multitude of noisy Londoners and their regular continental visitors. Established colonies of merchants from Normandy and Germany were already well settled in premises on either side of the Wallbrook where it ran into the Thames. Wool, hides, and grain were the principal British exports, and timber and cloth, fish, wine and pepper the most important imports.

It was the Norman Conquest which really took Britain into the mainstream of European trade and culture. William already ruled one of the wealthiest and best-organised kingdoms of western Europe, extending from Boulogne to Vannes and across to Mantes. One of his kinsmen, Robert Guiscard, ruled another as powerful and prosperous in the south, where he had subdued Sicily and part of Italy. To England William brought the administrators who were to increase its commercial prosperity and the architects and builders who were to create a city port worthy of this new destiny. The first priority was a series of defence works, of which the Tower of London was the most ambitious; by 1078 the White Tower had been completed and it is still there today. The whole Tower complex was completed by about 1300 and by that time the new rulers had completed a major reconstruction of the whole City. Barges came in continuous procession from Caen with pale Norman limestone, and others up-river from Kent with rough ragstone. While the White Tower was going up, a fire destroyed the church which the Saxons had raised at the highest point of the hill within the City walls. In its place, in 1087, under Norman inspiration, the first St Paul's Cathedral was built. It was the longest church in northern Europe and it had the highest spire — 450 feet — until it was destroyed by lightning in 1561.

The White Tower was symbolic of the physical safety of the City, and St Paul's of its spiritual well-being. Then it was time to look to bread-and-butter matters and so, in 1176, in the reign of Henry II, work began on a permanent London Bridge. This was no mere thoroughfare across the river, but rather a centre of the commercial life of the City. Besides the paved carriageway across the river there was an almost incredible assortment of buildings: houses and shops, even a church. The bridge was built further downstream than today's London Bridge, close to Billingsgate, at the site of the early ferry and, we assume of earlier timber bridges. Gifts were solicited to meet the cost of the bridge; the king and the Archbishop of Canterbury set generous examples, which others doubtless considered it prudent to follow, and the rest of the money was collected in the form of a tax on wool. This bridge, over many centuries, was patched, repaired and reconstructed. In 1758 it was transformed by the removal of all its ancient buildings, so that the width of the carriage-way could be trebled, in an effort to relieve congestion. Essentially, however, it remained the same bridge: the meeting place of everyone in London, the heart of all market activity, the arrival point of travellers from overseas or from the country. Always it was the scene of bustle and excitement and its history became embroidered with the folk-lore and legend of old London.

London Bridge was constructed with 20 arches, carried on 19 piers (or sterlings) resting on piles of oak or elm. The central arch, larger than the others, carried the Chapel of St Thomas. Another consisted of a drawbridge, so that larger vessels would be able to proceed up-stream without dismasting; this intention was ill-judged and in 1577, after long disuse, the drawbridge was replaced by a permanent arch incorporating a large black-and-white timber-framed building. There was one characteristic of the bridge, which could hardly have been foreseen, that had enormous long-term significance for the Port of London. The bridge was 930 feet in length, but, as each of its 19 piers was 20 feet wide, the movement of the tides was compressed into little more than half the total width of the river. In later centuries the problems were accentuated when three arches were permanently blocked up and water-wheels were installed under seven others to raise water and to grind corn. Eventually, there was only 143 feet width of navigable water altogether: 46 feet under the great arch, 62 feet under five arches to the south side of it, and 35 feet under three arches to the north. The consequence was that whirlpools and rapids were created in the river and at certain states of the tide the bridge became a weir, with a difference of five feet in the water levels on either side of it. Negotiation of this hazard became one of the special skills of Thames watermen, who earned a good living by discharging vessels moored in the Pool and carrying their cargoes to quays above the bridge. Sensible passengers travelling by river disembarked at one side of the bridge and rejoined their boats at the other; even so, over the centuries many lives were lost in the swirling waters. George Borrow was in time to bequeath us a dramatic description. In *Lavengro*, published in 1851, he wrote:

> "If upon the bridge there was a confusion, below it there was a confusion ten times confounded. The tide, which was fast ebbing, poured beneath the arches with a fall of several feet, forming in the river below as many whirlpools as there were arches. Truly tremendous was the roar of the descending waters, and the bellow of the tremendous gulfs . . ."

Although most of the arriving vessels moored in the Pool, much of the activity of the early port was above the bridge, at three principal quays: Bridewell, along the Fleet inlet, which was large enough to take a dozen ships at a time; Dowgate, on the Wallbrook, where the Easterlings built their guildhall and warehouse on one side of a large wedge-shaped basin, while the Norman traders established themselves on the opposite side; and Queenhithe, about mid-way between the other two, where a semi-circular basin had been cut into the muddy bank — this was the old "Aetheredes hyd" of 899 renamed when Henry I made it over as a gift to his queen, Matilda. Apart from these three inlets from the river, where vessels could berth and place cargo directly on to the quays, there were moorings down the centre of the stream from the Fleet to Wallbrook and cargo was transferred ashore by rowing boats. In a favoured position below the bridge, there was Billingsgate: a big V-shaped basin, with large open quays.

Between the twelfth and the sixteenth centuries the river port expanded steadily, until the whole of the northern bank between the Fleet and the Tower was occupied by wharves, warehouses and associated business premises. Some of the wharves were named after their owners, some had names which indicated the types of cargo they handled. One of the earliest and most interesting of them was Botolphs Wharf, just below the bridge, which was the point of arrival for all travellers coming by river boat from Gravesend. This included many from the continent and a large and lively "public kitchen" served food of every kind and quality to the travel-weary. Galley Quay was another area of special interest; there, as the name suggests, the great galleys from Venice and Genoa berthed, the biggest vessels of their time, with oars and sail, and carrying much exotic merchandise from the Orient. The names of many wharves changed from time to time. A fifteenth century list, starting at the Fleet and moving down-river, read: Watergate, Castle Baynard Dock, Woodwharf, Paul's Wharf, Fish Wharf, Broken Wharf, Saltwharf, Queenhithe, Garlickhithe, Wine Wharf, Dowgate and the Steelyard, Haywharf, Wolsies

Gate, Ebbgate, Oyster Gate, another Fish Wharf, Fresh Wharf, Botolphs Wharf, Lyon Quay, Billingsgate, Galley Quay and Tower Wharf. A map of 1560 adds Somers Quay (between Lyon Quay and Billingsgate) and Smarez Quay and Andrew Morice Quay near the Tower.

The City itself, at the north end of London Bridge, was still contained comfortably within the area of the old Roman walls, though these were no longer intact. A main thoroughfare ran from the bridge to Bishopsgate, passing the area where the Roman forum had stood. A little to the west, between this street and St Paul's Cathedral, there was an extensive open space: Cheapside, the City's principal market-place, scene of public pageants and punishments. It was lined with small shuttered shops and stalls, behind which were warehouses. From Cheapside another principal street ran back to the river at Dowgate, crossing busy Thames Street on the way. Between these principal thoroughfares there was a network of narrow streets and alleys, and in these the City artisans and craftsmen had their workshops and their wood-and-plaster, thatched homes. William FitzStephen, a monk born in London in 1118, provided a colourful description of this city; he wrote of craftsmen at their benches, apprentices practising archery, ladies at their spinning wheels, priests at their devotions in monasteries with beautiful gardens and orchards, students in schools, public cook-shops. He told us that the Thames sparkled and teemed with fish. Carried away with enthusiasm, he went on poetically:

"To this city merchants bring in Wares by Ships from every Nation under Heaven. The Arabian sends his Gold, the Sabean his Frankincense and Spices, the Scythian Arms, Oil of Palms from the plentiful wood, Babylon her far Soils, and Nilus his precious Stones, the Seres send purple Garments, they and Norway and Russia Trouts, Furs and Sables, and the French their wines."

Outside the City walls, it was open country to the east, with farms and small-holdings, and windmills turning wherever there were streams through the meadows. Bread for the medieval citizens arrived each day through the Aldgate and Bishopsgate entrances.

Characteristics of an affluent "west end" were also appearing as long ago as this. William of Normandy had found a royal palace at Westminster and had extended it. Around the Court noblemen and bishops built themselves fine town houses. The Bishops of Durham had one there as early as 1099 and, in the years that followed, all the best sites close to the river were used for splendid residences, until the vista of palaces and gardens presented to the traveller shooting London Bridge was breath-taking and without equal outside the Mediterranean. Westminster grew until it extended to within a mile of the City of London. Until the fourteenth century there was nothing but a rough

An early merchantman. The carrack was the merchant vessel of Tudor times. It had a large spread of canvas and elaborate castles and was usually of about 600 tons. This engraving by W. Master dates from about 1470. *Courtesy Trustees of the National Maritime Museum*

footpath along the river strand; then, during Richard II's reign, it was cleared and paved and became The Strand.

Development on the south bank of the river was of a different kind. The Bishops of Winchester had chosen to establish their palace in this unfashionable quarter and an important City church stood on the site of an earlier Nunnery of St Mary Overy ("of the ferry"? — certainly the nuns had oversight and profit of the ferry). This substantial ecclesiastical presence, however, did little to soften the essentially rough, if not brutal, flavour of life on the south side. It was a dingy muddle of fishermen's and boatmen's dwellings, liberally sprinkled with taverns and whore-houses.

The Port was at the heart of developing London and there were very few whose lives were not touched directly by port activities. From the earliest times the idea took root that port and City were one integrated whole. The port was not seen as a physical arrangement of wharves and cranes and warehouses and carts, but as the heart of a commercial system concerned with the purchase and marketing of commodities, with quality checks, with packaging and movement and storage, with insurance and credit financing. The range of talents involved was very wide and the pattern was set which would create, over many centuries, a mighty *entrepot*.

Originally, ownership of the Thames quays seems to have been a matter of royal whim. Henry I made a gift of Aetheredes Hithe to his wife and renamed it Queenhithe. Henry III ordered his Constable of the Tower to arrest ships of the Cinque Ports if they tried to discharge corn or fish other than at Queenhithe. The collection of tolls was a substantial source of royal income. The church, too, had its share; in the twelfth century the Fleet Hythe was held by the Dean and Chapter of St Paul's.

The export which provided London with its earliest flow of wealth was English wool, recognised as the finest raw material by the weavers of Flanders and northern Italy. The great monasteries were middle-men between wool farmers and merchants until the middle of the fourteenth century. Many foreign merchants based in London were there at the pleasure of the Court, which secured real advantage from having admitted them. Thus, the Easterlings had settled from 979, when Aethelred first granted them rights. They had strengthened their influence generation by generation and a time came, during the reign of Henry VII (1485-1509) when they were exporting in their vessels forty times more English wool and woollen cloth than went abroad in English ships. In the wake of William of Normandy, large numbers of merchants from Flanders and from Rouen arrived and set up in business. During the thirteenth century the Lombards arrived from northern Italy, settled in an area near present-day Lombard Street, and before long were handling all such wool cargoes as by-passed the Easterlings. Gradually the Lombards switched the emphasis of their activities to money-lending, but they were ceaselessly haggling with English rulers to secure trading privileges in return for loans, though they did not invariably get the better of the bargains. The thirteenth century kings, in particular, were prodigal with pledges when they required cash, but sometimes failed to redeem them. Several Italian banking families were ruined in the process, as also were some early London capitalists who made loans against promises that they might acquire a monopoly in wool exports.

The power and prodigality of the Court, the wealth of the Church and the influence of the foreign immigrants caused displeasure, jealousy, resentment and occasionally bitter fury among the native merchants of the City of London. As each king came to the throne, from William of Normandy onward, the City sought and was granted a charter, and the negotiations at the beginning of each reign represented a fierce struggle for power. By the twelfth century the City Guilds, which had first come into existence in Saxon times, had been re-organised for specifically trade purposes and were growing rich and ambitious. Some were recognised by royal charters, one of the privileges of which was that their freemen might adorn themselves in splendid robes; hence they became "livery companies". Some of them managed well enough without the royal licence, and instead had their regulations confirmed by the Mayor and Alderman of the City — once the City Corporation had come into existence in 1191, when the merchants seized their opportunity while Richard I was away on a Crusade. They elected from among the freemen of each Guild or Company aldermen to administer each of the wards into which the City was divided, and they met weekly. When the king came home, the new Corporation presented its demands and he was compelled to make significant concessions. Formal control of the river, which had previously been in the charge of the King's Officer in charge of the Tower, passed to the City Corporation. The representatives of the king who concerned themselves with the trade of the port agreed to liaise with a committee which represented various City interests. Many benefits which had flowed to the Court were progressively re-directed towards the City. As an example, the busy wharves at Queenhithe, where the tolls had kept successive queens in pocket-money, were leased to the Mayor and Citizens of London at an annual rent of £50. When a new and important cargo began to arrive in the Thames — coal shipped from the north-east coastal ports — the City gained immediate benefit. The first reference is in 1306 and the following year Edward I authorised the City to levy a sixpenny toll on each ship-load passing under London Bridge, for a period of three years, to help meet the cost of its maintenance and repair.

The whole system of tolls and duties, which had been brought into existence by royal whim, was due for revision. In 1275, in the earliest statute authorising the Crown to levy Customs duty, Edward I exchanged what had come to be regarded as "ancient and lawful custom" for specific duties of half a mark on every sack of wool and one mark on every last of leather and he appointed regular collectors of the revenue. The first Customs House was erected in 1382 at Wool Wharf, east of the site of the present building, and for the first few years the Comptroller of the Petty Customs there was Geoffrey Chaucer, the author of *The Canterbury Tales*, who earlier, in 1374, had been responsible for Customs control of wool, skins and leather. Wool was the main British export. It was collected in London, much of it brought by sea in coastal vessels which, after the formalities had been completed, sailed out of the Thames again in convoy across the Channel to Calais. This activity was concentrated in August, after the shearing, and in December, when the fells (fleeces) had been collected after the autumn slaughter of animals (for which, in those days, there was inadequate fodder).

The institution known as the Staple simplified the collection of duties. All principal (staple) commodities to be exported had to pass through the Staple, which during most of its history was situated in Calais, a town that for over two hundred years was English territory and conveniently close to the Flemish weavers. London was granted the right of "scavage", which meant that it supervised all packing for export, including weighing, grading, packing and sealing of the goods to be despatched to the Staple on the other side of the Channel. The wool was weighed at the King's Beam and Customs and subsidies were assessed at the Lead Hall in Mark Lane. Export merchants were charged special duties by the City Packer. Merchants who engaged in this trade formed the Company of the Staple, a corporate body of 300 to 400, with a monopoly of the trade with the Low Countries (the Italians were still permitted to dominate the trade with their country). Most of the 35,000 sacks of wool which were exported each year went to Flanders which, with Florence, was a centre of fine cloth-making in Europe. The system inevitably created some of the familiar evils of monopoly. Merchants of the Staple tried to buy cheaply and to sell expensively and this, in turn, called forth some strange remedies; for a short period the export of wool and the import of cloth was actually forbidden, and Flemish weavers were encouraged to come to work in England — which many of them did.

By a series of statutes over the centuries some of the worst abuses of the earlier usury were ended. In 1344 ecclesiastics were forbidden to engage in commerce. During the reign of Edward IV (1461-1484) the City cancelled a large part of a debt owed to it by the king in exchange for a charter confirming that it possessed all rights of packing of woollen cloth, skins and all other goods requiring to be packed in barrels or anywise to be enclosed, plus all oversight of the examination of customable merchandise arriving in London by land or water. The City was granted, too, rights to all porterage of merchandise between the Thames and the warehouses of foreign merchants, all sorting and grading of spices and other merchandise, and all carriage of wines between the port and the vintners' cellars.

Although they had no choice but to work in close co-operation with the foreign merchants based in London, the City entrepreneurs kept a wary eye upon them at all times and sometimes there were open clashes; on such occasions the street population was roused to chauvinistic chanting and there were ugly scenes. The complaints against the foreigners were the familiar ones that they bought themselves privileges, that they tried to corner commodities, and that they took over the best dwellings and forced up rents. In 1483, for example, the merchants from Venice, Lucca, Florence, Genoa and Catalonia were under attack because they were alleged to have cornered goods, made excessive gains and then remitted all the proceeds to their home cities. Richard III, seeking to mollify the complainants, decreed that the Italians should deal only wholesale and should be compelled to spend their profits on English goods.

The foreigners, however, brought many benefits to London because of their long-established contacts with all the trading centres of the known world. The experience of the Easterlings illustrates the "love-hate" relationship which the City had with all foreigners as century followed century. The Germans first arrived, as we have seen, at the invitation of King Aethelred in 979. They were a small, independent group of merchants from the Rhine. At that time all Baltic trade, including that which flowed to and from Novgorod, the great trading centre of northern Russia, was focused on eastern Sweden, and the Easterlings controlled the shipping routes across the North Sea. In 1241 the merchants of Hamburg and Lubeck formed the Hanseatic League, which absorbed the Swedish association and, later, the Easterlings in London, whose headquarters was then designated one of the four principal Hanseatic League "factories" — the others were in Bruges, Bergen and Novgorod. The London association monopolised the import into Britain of all the products of northern Europe: timber, masts, pitch and tar, cables and ropes, flax and hemp. They handled, too, the spices which came from the Orient by overland routes across Russia. They exported grain, cloth and wool. And they supplemented their trading activities by banking operations, including a series of loans to indigent English kings.

During the reign of Henry II (1154-1189) the Easterlings established their headquarters in a *Gildhalla Teutonicorum* at Dowgate. It was both their guildhall and their warehouse and it became known to Londoners as The Steelyard. By the time of Richard II, two centuries later, they had taken over an adjoining property, "a great house with a large wharf on the Thames". In 1598 John Stowe described their premises as "large, built of stone, with three arched gates towards the street, the middlemost whereof is far bigger than the others and is seldom opened, and the other two are mured up". For a long time the Easterlings used only their own ships, but by the beginning of the fourteenth century they were having to concede something of this monopoly. The first record of a London-owned trading ship, in 1315, indicates that it was carrying a cargo of 120 half-sacks of wool, valued at £1,200, to Antwerp on behalf of three of the Hansa merchants. In 1551 the Steelyard merchants were under particularly fierce attack and during the reign of Edward VI their privileges were severely cut back. During the reign of Elizabeth their troubles multiplied as London merchants developed a new, aggressive confidence. For a time the queen sent Germans and Lombards back to their homelands and an English Merchant Adventurers' Company, incorporated in London in 1553, quickly seized their advantage and created a tight monopoly of their own. This was no improvement for the country at large, as was indicated by a communication from Lord Burleigh to the Lord Chancellor in 1587 recommending that, in order to break the Merchant Adventurers' monopoly, the men of the Steelyard should have their privileges restored and foreigners in general should again be permitted to trade in wool. The quarrel was made up and the Easterlings returned to their Thames-side premises, though their influence in the port was never re-established on the earlier scale. In 1598 Elizabeth took firm action to prevent their re-acquiring monopoly privileges.

The Steelyard was destroyed in the Great Fire of 1666, but when Thames Street was rebuilt four years later the German merchants continued to operate from new warehouses on the same site. In later years, gradually they left and their premises were let to others, but the building itself continued to be owned by the cities of Lubeck, Hamburg and Bremen until 1853, when it was sold to the former Victoria Dock Company with the assent of these cities. It was pulled down in 1863 to make way for Cannon Street railway station.

Whatever the stresses and strains of the dramatically evolving society during the period of about five hundred years from William the Conqueror to Queen Elizabeth I—the constant tension and the frequent conflict between Court and City, between native and foreigner, between competing merchants —the progressive expansion of trade provided sufficient wealth for everyone to do well. The full trading potentialities of a European market were exploited and the port of London, with Antwerp, was at the centre of the flood. The stage had been set for the emergence of Britain as the greatest mercantile nation in the world.

Nowhere could one sense the atmosphere of confidence and enterprise more keenly than on the river. It was the shop-window of London's prosperity. It was always thickly crowded with shipping. Apart from the merchantmen from all the major ports of Europe and the constant procession of coasters which formed the most important element in the domestic transport system, there were 40,000 watermen working between Windsor and Gravesend in Elizabeth's time—and for long afterwards. Everyone travelled by river craft.

From time to time, the routine dramas of daily life were enhanced by glittering pageantry. Great occasions of state were celebrated on the Thames. Magnificent painted barges, with decorative awnings and flying standards, and with liveried crews, were used by the Court, by Parliament and by the City. They were accompanied by guard boats which glowed and glittered as the sun caught the uniforms of yeomen and the cold steel of their halberds. Royal progresses, the Lord Mayor's show, the reception of distinguished foreign visitors: all were staged on the river. Tournaments were fought on it and spectacular firework displays raised above it. Maitland has left us an eye-witness account of the coronation of Anne Boleyn in 1533, when she arrived by boat at Westminster in a procession which included 50 sumptuous barges, each with its own band playing, carrying the Lord Mayor, Aldermen and Commons dressed in scarlet gowns and gold chains:

"Leading the line, in front of the City Barge, was another which was mounted with Ordnance and the Statues of Savages, Dragons and other monstrous Creatures which incessantly emitted Noise, Smoke and Fire. Then the City Barge, attended on the Right by the Haberdashers' State Barge, called the Batchelors, which was covered with golden brocades, and at its Yards silken sails appendant, with two rich Standards of the King's and Queen's Arms at her Head and Stern, besides an agreeable variety of Streamers and Flags, containing the Companies' Arms and those of the Merchant Adventurers; and the Shrouds and Ratlines being hung with a number of small Bells produced a Pleasant Noise; and on the left was a Barge which contained a beautiful Mount, on which stood a white Falcon, crowned, perching on a golden Stump, encircled with Red and White roses, being the Queen's Emblem; and round the Mount sat divers beautiful Virgins, singing and playing melodiously. Then followed the other Barges in pleasant order, according to their Station and proper Distances, in which beautiful order they proceeded below Greenwich."

Such Thames theatre cost fortunes, but the City felt that it could afford it. There was a sense of a New World opening up, as indeed was literally the case. London was poised, prepared, peremptory as it faced its destiny as the great world port.

CHAPTER THREE

The Age of Expansion

ON 10th August, 1497 a Venetian mariner named John Cabot arrived in London to report to King Henry the Seventh on a voyage which he had completed at Bristol four days earlier. The King had granted him a licence to explore in the north Atlantic and the merchants of Bristol had provided the funds for his fleet. Cabot had thereupon made the first northern crossing since the Vikings (though, in the state of knowledge at the time, it was believed to be the first ever). His landfall had been in either Newfoundland or Nova Scotia – he did not know precisely where he had been. He had a clear belief, however, that he had discovered a New World and the narrative of his adventures was embellished with aspirations for the future which must have fired the imagination of the City merchants with whom he talked. They were already infected by a restless spirit of wonder and curiosity, fed by a spate of travel and adventure books coming from the novel new printing presses which Caxton and others had set up. Some of the authors offered more fiction than fact, but in an age of superstition it was difficult to define where one merged into the other; it was undeniable that wonderful new explorations into unknown seas and continents were being accomplished.

Cabot had brought much interesting information with him when he had first arrived in England in 1495. He was one of a generation of master sailors which grew up in Venice and Genoa during the catastrophic period for those city republics which followed the fall of Constantinople to the Turks in 1453. Mediterranean trade fell completely into Moslem hands, the ships which had carried the riches of the Orient to Western Europe lay moored in harbour, and the finest seamen of Venice and Genoa had little choice but to emigrate. They arrived in Spain and Portugal as those countries, also denied free movement in the Mediterranean, were turning their eyes towards the Atlantic. Cabot went first to Spain, as did his fellow Genoese, Christopher Columbus. He was there when the news came of Columbus' pioneer ocean crossing and, a few years later, of the first rounding of the southern cape of Africa by the Portuguese, Bartholomew Dias.

As a visitor to England, then, John Cabot enjoyed the mystical aura of a man who had returned from a voyage beyond the edge of the known world,

The Thames Waterman. This Rowlandson cartoon depicting a group of watermen soliciting custom at Wapping conveys something of the boisterous atmosphere of the old port.

Courtesy P.L.A.

but he was also a source of much practical knowledge of the activities and plans of other great maritime nations. He stayed in London for a fortnight, probably met most of the influential men of the time, and, though he then returned to Bristol, must have profoundly influenced attitudes and ambitions in the capital.

No-one could have apprehended, as the fifteenth century ran towards its close, how the explosion of knowledge was about to transform the lives of men and nations. Londoners were well aware of some of the interesting and important changes taking place: vessels were getting bigger every year and their design greatly improved; compasses and other aids to navigation were more reliable; luxury goods becoming available to the rich spread a new awareness of territories and seas which awaited exploration. But only with hindsight can we appreciate how, during the fifteenth and sixteenth centuries, there came to maturity a number of scientific advances and technological developments which, taken together, have never been outclassed by any related sequence of human achievements. During these two centuries men first discovered that their world was a globe which could be circum-navigated, they learned how to make such voyages, and they explored and exploited new continents until an entirely new pattern of world trade had been established. No-one seized the new opportunities more energetically or more shrewdly than the merchants, the sailors and the bankers of London.

Before the fifteenth century, time was measured in Europe with half-hour sandglasses and, after dark, with a simple instrument called a *nocturnal* which derived approximate information from the stars. Speed and distance covered were largely guess-work; the only method of measurement involved throwing a piece of timber overboard at the prow and estimating the time a vessel took to pass it. The best maps were still those produced about the middle of the second century by a Helenised Egyptian named Ptolemy. Mathematics were in such a rudimentary state that accounts of ships' stores and logs of mileages run were often kept in Roman numerals. In a world of such limited knowledge, navigation as a science was unknown. Most sailors were happy only when there was a coastline in sight.

New theories were evolved slowly and were applied piecemeal by the more adventurous. Each discovery opened the way to others; astronomers, mathematicians, cartographers and instrument makers expanded the frontiers of their various sciences and only then discerned that their efforts were inter-related. The builders of ships and the men who sailed in them adapted to the new facts as they were proven, but none too readily. They were conservative, suspicious of book learning, uninterested in theory. They put their faith in practical experience and traditional skills. Faced with large-scale innovation, the average citizen of the late fifteenth century was remarkably like his descendants of the late eighteenth or late twentieth centuries.

There are always, however, pioneers who know how to seize chances. When the Vikings sailed southward using a simple "lodestone" compass, there were Normans who immediately understood its significance, introduced it to the Mediterranean fleets, and dispersed the idea of sailing out of sight of land and *crossing* the seas. This called for a different kind of vessel; ships without decks propelled by oars were unsuitable for rough water and provided neither sufficient space nor protection for long-distance cargoes. New vessels were evolved, with covered holds, sails, and rudders. By the sixteenth century they had developed to the merchant *carracks* and the fighting *galleons*: great vessels of up to one thousand tons, with castles and large spreads of canvas. Two distinct early traditions of shipbuilding, the Scandinavian and the Mediterranean, had blended by about 1450 in a basic barque design which set the pattern for the age of discovery. In the thirteenth century the universal freighting vessel in northern waters was the *knorr*, derivative from the Viking longboat, with a single deck and a single sail. Its straight keel was a great advantage in the Thames, where it could take the ground without strain at ebb tides. Castles were later added at bow and stern, the hold was enlarged, and in its ultimate development the vessel became known as the *cog*. These were the ships most familiar to Londoners; but there were others of a different kind. The Mediterranean tradition produced a short, chunky hull and a lateen sail, often with a second mast, and from about 1300 the Venetians built in their state dockyards and chartered to their merchants the *great galley*, a three-masted vessel which used sail at sea but was manoeuvred in and out of harbour by oarsmen. For over two hundred years, until 1532, these vessels were seen in the Thames at the time of the annual Venetian convoy to northern Europe. The shipbuilders of the Atlantic ports of Spain and Portugal absorbed the best features of the northern and Mediterranean vessels and developed a hybrid type during the fourteenth and fifteenth centuries: multi-masted stern-ruddered cargo boats with several sails and greatly increased cargo capacity.

These were the vessels which traded out of London during Tudor years and for long after. Most of the *carracks*, which were the big merchantmen, were of about 600 tons, with elaborate after-castles, square-rigged on fore and main masts and with a lateen-rigged mizzen mast. Topsails were added by the mid-sixteenth century. At the other extreme, coastal trade was handled by *caravels*, vessels of 70 to 80 feet overall and usually not above 60 to 70 tons. They had a single deck, a modest raised poop and a transome stern, with two, three or sometimes even four masts. Between the *carrack* and the *caravel* there was a variety of intermediate types of from 100 to 300 tons.

Britain came relatively late to the business of ship-building, and there was no established tradition in the Thames before the fifteenth century. When the first yards were established, they were concerned with fighting ships. In 1475 Edward the Fourth fitted out on the Thames a fleet large enough to carry

1,500 men and 15,000 archers to an invasion of France. Henry the Seventh built there the first vessel of 1,000 tons, the *Henry Grâce à Dieu*. Henry the Eighth set up royal dockyards at Deptford and Woolwich in 1515, to supplement a yard established earlier at Portsmouth, and he created the Admiralty to organise the Navy as a distinct and separate service. He lived long enough to see a navy of 45 vessels, including fifteen galleons, and to believe that, for the first time, England was secure from invasion from the Continent. In the wake of the dockyards there came numerous other shipbuilding yards and so long as vessels were built of timber — that is well into the nineteenth century — the yards prospered. A Shipwrights' Company was established in London in 1612, the year in which the famous Blackwall shipyard was established. For nearly three centuries this yard built East Indiamen and vessels for the Royal Navy.

As larger vessels of improved design took to the water, men learned to sail them more efficiently. By the fifteenth century the rudimentary compasses of the Vikings had evolved to much more accurate ones produced by professional instrument-makers. The earliest quadrant had been invented, so that latitude could be calculated. By the early sixteenth century the cross-staff, which offered a rough-and-ready way of determining longitude, came into use. From early in the fifteenth century there had been pilot-books, in which the men who sailed the known coast-lines recorded their observations and estimates of distances, depths and tides, but the general use of such pilot-books (as well as of Arabic number-writing techniques) was limited until the invention of

Watermen wore silver arm badges. The one shown here was part of the uniform of watermen employed by the Commercial Dock Company in 1820. Reproduced actual size 3¾ × 3¼ inches. *Courtesy P.L.A.*

printing made knowledge more widely available and encouraged ships' masters, among others, to learn to read. Pilotage gave way to navigation only after the publication in 1551 of a manual prepared by a Spaniard, Martin Cortes, but even then it remained for long the preserve of an aristocracy of experts. The knowledge of an accurate mathematical formula enabling a ship's position to be fixed precisely, so that dead-reckoning could be dispensed with, did not come until the eighteenth century, but along the route to that discovery there were many milestones and a growing confidence. In 1484 a commission of mathematicians in Portugal, seeking a method of establishing latitude by solar observation, produced tables of declination. In 1543 Copernicus propounded that the sun was the centre of the solar system, and by the end of that century there were charts giving a grid of latitudes and longitudes and representing the earth's curved surface on a flat sheet with a mathematically consistent projection. Soon after that, Dutch spectacle-makers stumbled upon the principles of optical magnification, and in 1632 Galileo established the daily and annual movements of the earth round the sun. In 1675 Charles the Second sought to make an English contribution when he established the Royal Observatory at Greenwich, to assist the quest for a reliable method of determining positions at sea. The significant discovery was made, however, by a German, Johannes Kepler, in the early years of the eighteenth century: he revolutionised astronomical calculations when he defined precisely how the planets orbit the sun.

The London which John Cabot visited in 1497 buzzed with excitement and curiosity. It was at the centre of the known world, poised between northern Europe and the Mediterranean; now, suddenly, it comprehended that it lay between that old world and a new one with incalculable possibilities. Inhibiting superstitions were being dispelled; if Dias had sailed to the southern cape of Africa, then patently it could not be true that the sea boiled at the Equator. Immediately, there was an important practical task to be undertaken and Spain, Portugal and the Netherlands — as well as England — dedicated themselves to this task. In all these countries the rich had developed a taste for the Oriental exotica which had been imported from Venice and Genoa: silks and cotton cloth, precious stones and the whole range of what were termed "spices" — a blanket word which covered drugs, dyes, perfumes, unguents, cosmetics, foods and condiments. Some of them were used as preservatives or as flavouring for what might otherwise have been unpalatable, and they were consequently now regarded as essentials. A fourteenth century merchants' handbook listed 288 different "spices", not only including such things as peppers, cinnamon, nutmegs and cloves, but also sugar, waxes and gums.

It was known that these things had come from Constantinople to Venice and some understood that they had reached Constantinople in dhows sailing up the Red Sea or by camel caravans across the deserts from Oriental countries called China, India and Ceylon. Now Constantinople was closed to the west, the supplies had been cut off, and not only the merchants but the consumers felt themselves deprived. A new route to the Orient had to be found.

The Portuguese scored the first success. Ten years after Dias had rounded the Cape, his fellow-countryman Vasco da Gama reached Calicut on the Malabar coast, and by 1501 the first consignment of eastern spices shipped via Lisbon reached the European market in Antwerp. Spanish fleets, taking the same direction as Columbus, diligently explored the coastline of South America until, in 1520, Ferdinand Magellan led his fleet of five merchant ships through the straits which bear his name into the Pacific Ocean. A second new route to the Orient had been opened, and by that same year Spain had also claimed Mexico and most of the West Indian islands.

No matter how keen merchants and mariners might be, exploration required royal patronage and, until Elizabeth came to the throne in 1559, England had too many religious and political preoccupations to compete effectively. The merchants, however, busied themselves in other ways. They developed a sophisticated system of maritime assurance and they took over most of the profitable banking functions which had earlier been performed by foreign immigrants. Out of the ferment of the times emerged a society which was more flexible and far-seeing, more responsive and resilient, better attuned to the new opportunities opened up by the new learning and the enlarged horizons than any other in Europe. Catholic Spain remained a military and hierarchical state, grown rich and complacent on the treasures it had plundered from the New World but lacking mercantile flair and financial organisation. These were precisely the skills that London had developed. A tradition of individual enterprise and generous reward was established in the City, which enjoyed prosperity and grew. Between 1500 and 1600 the population of London increased from 50,000 to 200,000.

When the time came to direct English energies to a drive for a share of the overseas territories and trade, London was rich, strong and ambitious. Ironically, it concentrated most of its effort upon what proved to be an impossible objective: the discovery of yet another new route to the Orient. An English merchant, Robert Thorne, explained in 1527: "There is one way to discover, which is into the North. For out of Spain they have discovered all the Indies and seas occidental, and out of Portugal all the Indies and seas oriental". It was the penalty on the late-comer and it seemed logical, but the icy seas north of the Russian and Canadian land-masses had a fatal attraction. The efforts which followed were dogged, persistent, characterised by great courage and endurance, but they were doomed to failure.

The prospects of the northwest and northeast passages, argued interminably, formed a favourite intellectual exercise of the Elizabethans. During the winter of 1565-66 the Queen herself listened earnestly to a staged debate

31

An early enclosed dock. The Howland Great Dock, completed before 1700, offered ten acres of sheltered water and was the first big wet dock open to all shipping. This 1720 engraving is by Thomas Badeslade.   *Courtesy Trustees of the Museum of London*

between two protagonists: Sir Humphrey Gilbert, a half-brother of Raleigh, pressing the case for the northwest route, and Anthony Jenkinson, who had actually sailed to Russia and crossed it to the Caspian, favouring the northeast passage. Both were utterly convinced that their preferred route was much shorter than those to the south and that they would be able to undercut Spanish and Portuguese freight charges.

The first major expedition from London was in 1553. Sir Hugh Willoughby sailed with three ships fitted at Deptford, hoping to reach Cathay by a northeast passage. Willoughby himself, and two of his ships, were lost but a party led by his second-in-command, Richard Chancellor, reached Archangel and pressed on to Moscow on sledges. Chancellor negotiated there a trading agreement which opened the way for the establishment in 1555 of the Muscovy Company. Sebastian Cabot, a son of the Cabot who had first come to Britain in 1495, advised on the formation of this company and was its first governor, and City merchants subscribed for 240 shares of £25 each to provide its capital. This was the first of a series of such merchant adventurer companies formed in London over a period of fifty years, their capital subscribed by individual shareholders. There was the Eastland Company, trading in the Baltic; the Merchant Adventurers' Company, trading in the North Sea; the Turkey (or Levant) Company, trading in the Mediterranean; the Africa Company, trading along the west coast of that continent; the Virginia Company, formed to develop the territory which today forms Maryland, Virginia and Carolina; the East India Company, and the West India Company, and the Hudson's Bay Company.

For well over seventy years the search continued for a northern route to the East. Sir Martin Frobisher tried the northwest passage three times: in 1576, 1577 and 1578. John Davis tried it three times: 1585, 1586 and 1587. Henry Hudson tried it in 1610, when his crew mutinied and set him adrift in a small boat to die. The dream did not perish, even then. A North West Company was formed, with 300 investors, including three of Hudson's mutineers and the Archbishop of Canterbury of the time. Not until 1631 was defeat accepted, by which time more lives had been lost than in any exploration of similar scale anywhere else in the world. The only worth-while discoveries were of cod and whales and seals, and the London merchant adventurers made the best of these products. Efforts to find a northeast passage proved equally dismal, but these were abandoned earlier—in 1580.

A year before that a treaty was signed between England and the Ottoman Sultan, permitting ships of the Levant Company to bring considerable quantities of eastern goods from Syrian ports, and in 1583 an English expedition led by Sir John Newbery and Ralph Fitch was sent overland on a commercial reconnaissance, carrying a letter of introduction from Queen Elizabeth to the Emperor of China. Newbery died on the trip and Fitch fell into the hands of the Portuguese. He escaped and made his way, through many of the markets and trading posts of the Middle East and the Persian Gulf, to Goa and the Mogul court in Agra. When eventually he found his way home to London in 1591 the information he brought, confirming other accounts circulating at the time about the wealth of the Indies trade, gave a great impetus to mercantile ambitions.

It was the firm conviction of each of the competing nations that whatever trade routes they discovered were theirs to exploit in perpetuity. Spain fought off contestants for the trade of the Americas and Portugal claimed an exclusive right to all trade from the East by the Cape route. For a time, the English and the Dutch avoided any direct challenge, the English still hopeful of discovering their own exclusive route, the Dutch busily taking over the majority of fright movement along the Atlantic coast of Europe—in the *fluyt** they had evolved a vessel that was virtually a floating hold, with the lowest operating costs anyone had ever achieved. Some Englishmen, impatient for results, tried direct action, particularly Sir Francis Drake, who was the central character in a continuous running battle with the Spaniards in the Caribbean from 1570 until England and Spain found themselves formally at war in 1585. Even Drake's programme included some serious exploration, for in 1577-80 he sailed around the world, prospecting the south-east routes to the Orient; Elizabeth met him at Deptford on his return to the Thames and knighted him on the deck of his *Golden Hind.*

The spirit of Drake was in the ascendant and now events began to move fast. With the defeat of the Armada in 1588, the power of Spain was broken. By 1591 Elizabeth was prepared to give her consent to a direct intrusion on the Portuguese route around the Cape. Sir James Lancaster led an expedition of three merchant vessels and, although only one of them returned safely (in 1594), this was effectively the end of the Portuguese monopoly in India. The Dutch, resolute not to lose ground, despatched 51 vessels to the Far East during the following three or four years, taking out German-manufactured arms and armour, toys, glass, linen and velvet and returning with the coveted spice cargoes. The London merchants accused the Dutch of seeking to corner supplies of pepper, and sought and obtained Elizabeth's permission to set up an East India Company. The Dutch almost immediately formed a rival East India Company and the stage was set for bitter competition which led, eventually, to war. By this time a view had formed in London that factory colonies and isolated settlements of the kind the Portuguese had possessed throughout the East were not satisfactory; permanent settlement of whole regions would be a better policy. The Dutch and the French were reaching much the same conclusion at the same time. In 1585 Sir Walter Raleigh tried to give practical expression to these new theories by planting an English colony on an island off the coast of Virginia, but these pioneers disappeared without

*A small rounded stern supply vessel shiprigged on three masts.

trace. When Elizabeth died in 1603, Spain and Portugal were still the only European nations with settled colonies on the other side of the Atlantic.

In the Port of London the pattern of increasing activity during Elizabeth's reign was determined by an Act which had been passed in 1558, the year before she became queen. A special commission selected 1,464 feet of riverside quays between London Bridge and the Tower, on the northern bank, and these were designated the Legal Quays. The purpose was to protect Customs revenue; Customs officers were installed at these quays and all cargoes, other than fish, had to be loaded or discharged at them. At the same time, other legislation obliged merchants to ship goods only in English vessels for a period of five years. A later Act (1663) listed twenty Legal Quays, as follows: Brewer's Quay (73 feet), Chester's Quay (51 feet), Galley Quay (101 feet), Wool Dock (61 feet), Custom House Quay (202 feet), Porter's Quay (103 feet), Ralph's Quay (81 feet), Dyce Quay (111 feet), Smart's Quay (27 feet), Somers' Quay (73 feet), Lion Quay (37 feet), Botolph Quay (78 feet), Hammond's Quay (23 feet), Gaunt's Quay (31 feet), Cocks Quay (41 feet), Fresh Wharf (140 feet) and Billingsgate Dock (172 feet). Most of them were named after their owners, and their names changed from time to time. Many of them could accommodate only one vessel at a time. Many specialised in particular kinds of cargoes; for example, Billingsgate handled fish, corn, salt, stones, victuals and fruit. The quays were divided one from another by river steps.

A 1757 caricature by Boitard entitled "Imports from France", showing cranes operated by treadmill and porterage using poles supported on shoulders.

Courtesy Trustees of the Museum of London

Access to the Legal Quays was from Thames Street, which was the longest and the busiest in the City during Elizabeth's reign, and, indeed, until the nineteenth century, the liveliest and most congested. It was a bewildering scene of activity as produce from every corner of the world daily crossed its cobbles. Road surfaces did not permit the use of wheeled trucks, and most cargoes arrived packed in barrels, which could be rolled over the quays. Otherwise, the port labourers had to carry them on their backs; the heavier ones were transported on poles between the shoulders of two men.

The river itself was a dense forest of masts and rigging. Many cargoes were loaded into or discharged from ships moored in the stream, the barges which served them nosing around their hulls like dark swamp monsters. Small coasting vessels flapped their sails in every open channel. Wherries with a few passengers in the care of whistling watermen criss-crossed the stream from bank to bank. Heavy barges brought thirty twopenny-fare passengers at a time to London Bridge from Gravesend, many of them travellers from the Continent. This was the "Long Ferry", which had run since 1293 at least, and the operation of which had, by royal favour, been the right of Gravesend men since 1401. There was also a "Short Ferry", from Gravesend to Tilbury. Between Limehouse and Westminster timber cargoes were discharged into the river itself, provided the necessary arrangements could be made with the Customs. The bridge remained the centre of all activity in the port. Eating houses and taverns offering accommodation were concentrated near the landing stage at Billingsgate.

The first coaches were introduced into England in Elizabeth's reign and, with road improvements, they became so popular that by 1600 the streets were jammed with them. The watermen fought them with much bitterness; a writer of the time complained that the carriage had "filched from honest boatmen 500 fares a day". But, in fact, the Thames remained the principal highway to and for London and development of the South Bank created much new traffic. Bankside, as it was called, was the pleasure park of the Elizabethans. The Paris Gardens, at its western extremity, was beyond the jurisdiction of the City and amphitheatres featuring bear-baiting and bull-baiting drew boisterous and dissolute crowds there. Afterwards they swilled ale in the taverns which stood in every street. Those with different tastes patronised some of the earliest London theatres, the Rose, the Swan, the Blackfriars, the Globe, and others, where the Elizabethan dramatists established their reputations. Shakespeare wrote many of his plays for the Globe, once it had been opened in 1599.

The London of 1600 was packed with a greatly-swollen population, enjoying a rough humour in its streets and ale-houses; it was producing a fine, creative drama which has never been surpassed; it was excited by tales of new and distant lands and peoples; it was bursting with confidence and ambition. The East India Company was a symbolic product of this age and this spirit; it became in time the most powerful of all European trading companies, the principal British shipping concern, and arguably the most powerful single influence on the development of the Port of London throughout its whole history.

The Lord Mayor of London summoned the leading City merchants to a meeting at Founders Hall in 1599 and a decision was made there to establish an association specifically to trade with India and the Far East. On the last day of 1599 Elizabeth signed the charter instituting "The Governor and Company of the Merchants of London trading into the East Indies." It was granted to George, the Earl of Cumberland, and 215 knights, aldermen and merchants who between them subscribed £72,000 in £25 shares. The original licence was for a term of fifteen years and the Company's initial operations were on a limited scale. It wound up its accounts and paid capital and dividends to each shareholder at the conclusion of each two-year voyage. The Company recruited crews for its fleets from among the Thames watermen. For the first voyage, which began at Woolwich on 13th February, 1601, a total of 480 were signed on, to man a fleet consisting of one vessel of 600 tons, one of 300 tons, two of 200 tons and one of 130 tons. Sir James Lancaster, who had prospected the route some years earlier, was in command. The first voyage was a considerable success, the ships returned full of spices, mainly pepper, and a second voyage followed almost immediately.

By 1611 the Company was into its stride. In that year it established a factory at Masulipatam, half-way up the east coast of India, and, prospecting from that base, Francis Day acquired for the company sovereignty of a strip of land in Madras on which he built Fort St George, the first fortified factory in India. In 1612 the Mogul Governor of Surat authorised the first English trading post in the dominions of the Grand Mogul. Surat, on the Tapti river in what is now Bombay province, was the chief port of the Mogul empire and it became the headquarters of the East India Company and continued as such until 1687, when a move was made to Bombay. The goodwill of the Grand Mogul was essential. His empire had blossomed under Akbar, a contemporary of Elizabeth in England, who became master of most of the Indian sub-continent and fostered a rich and progressive culture and a sound administration. His son, Jahangir, enlarged this empire and established a link, by marriage, with Persia. To his court at Agra went in 1615 Sir Thomas Roe, who has been described as "the first great Anglo-Indian statesman", and he remained there for three years doubling the roles of Ambassador of King James the First and Agent of the East India Company. The privileges he obtained for his London masters not only assured wealth for the East India investors; they may be said to have laid the foundations of the British Empire.

In London the East India Company made its headquarters at Blackwall and it completed offices and some residential accommodation and storehouses

Limehouse 1793. The port did not eliminate pastoral pleasures until well into the nineteenth century. When Robert Dodd painted this scene, windmills still stood along the western shore of the Isle of Dogs, cows grazed nearby, and it was a pleasant place for a stroll. Limehouse Church was known to seamen from all over the world. *Courtesy P.L.A.*

there in 1612. In the same year the shipyard and dry docks at Blackwall were established alongside. By 1620 the Company owned 10,000 tons of shipping and employed 2,500 mariners, 500 ships' carpenters and 120 factors. A glimpse of its operations in that year is provided by this table:

Imports to England	Cost on board ship in India	Selling price in London
250,000 lbs Pepper	£26,041	£208,333
150,000 lbs Cloves	5,126	45,000
150,000 lbs Nutmeg	2,500	18,750
50,000 lbs Mace	1,666	15,000
200,000 lbs Indigo	11,666	50,000
107,140 lbs China Raw Silk	37,499	107,140
50,000 pieces Calico	15,000	50,000
	£99,498	£494,223

The Company consolidated its position in India, but was less successful elsewhere, and the Portuguese fought savagely against the intruders. The Company made early forays into Indonesia, the Moluccas, and the other so-called Spice Islands, but by 1625 it was in retreat from them all and disposed to concentrate on India, where it had had the best of clashes with the Portuguese. European rivals remained a threat, however, and now the Mogul empire was beginning to break up. The Company decided that its factories required the protection of armed forces and in 1661 it was granted a charter authorising it to raise troops and maintain fortifications. Eventually, it had 24,000 troops in its pay and virtually controlled India, and it became as much an imperial administration as a commercial company. It built the cities of Bombay, Calcutta and Madras. The post of local manager at Surat evolved in course of time to that of President of Bombay, head of an executive government with its own taxation, law courts and standing army. None of this was bad for business, and wealth flowed back to London in an ever-broadening stream. Shareholders had good reason to raise their voices in praise at the special church services in London which marked the departure and homecoming of each fleet. The early system of raising capital for each separate voyage was replaced by operations for fixed terms of years and finally, in 1657, the East India Company raised permanent capital and became a joint stock company in the modern sense.

Equally dramatic events occurred in the west. Between the death of Elizabeth in 1603 and the Civil War in 1641, eighty thousand Englishmen crossed the Atlantic to settle in America. The first of them went to Jamestown to plant tobacco within a year of the Virginia Company getting its charter in 1606. Year by year this Company shipped out more emigrants, with supplies;

but the Company itself did not prosper and by 1623 was insolvent, whereupon its charter was revoked and Virginia became the first Crown Colony. The *Mayflower* arrived in New England with the Pilgrim Fathers in 1620 and within twelve years 20,000 English Puritans followed them. In 1629 a powerful syndicate of Puritans obtained a grant of land for settlement in New England and incorporated themselves by royal charter as the Massachussetts Bay Company, with headquarters in Boston. In 1663 eight influential public men secured a patent of proprietorship of the unoccupied coastline southward from Virginia to the Spanish territory of Florida — and thus Carolina was settled. Several of the West Indian islands were occupied early in the century and by 1640 sugar planting was successfully established. This new crop was of immense economic importance: by 1660 exports from Barbados to England were greater than exports from either Virginia or New England, and this relative balance was not disturbed throughout the seventeenth century.

A first Scottish settlement was established in Nova Scotia in 1627 and during the latter decades of the century the Hudsons Bay Company established a prosperous fur trade in the north. It would be an incomplete picture of British enterprise in the New World if mention were not made of the Africa Company which, from 1662, supplied the English plantations with black slaves; taking the year 1700 as an example, this Company shipped 25,000 of them.

So there was an explosion of world trade. London was the principal, though not the only, beneficiary. Court, Parliament and City each did its best to extract the maximum advantage. The idea of a mercantile economy took form. The colonies were to be regarded, in a sense, as part of the mother country. England would supply the colonists, the capital, the ships, the trading know-how, and the Royal Navy would provide defence. The colonies would supply Britain with raw materials and basic products, but would not compete with her manufactures. There would be a cosy monopoly of trade within the Empire. Thus, the Navigation Acts of 1650, 1651, 1660 and 1696 provided that no goods could be imported into or exported from any English colony except in English or colonial ships, and that certain "enumerated" commodities, particularly sugar and tobacco, could be shipped only to England or to another English colony. Foreign shipping was excluded entirely from the plantations. The Staple Act of 1663 provided that all goods, whether of English or foreign origin, had to be handled in an English port before being shipped to the eventual destination. The intention was clear: to create in Britain a vast entrepôt of trade, a clearing house for the products of most of the developed world. As a result, there was a spectacular expansion of the English merchant fleet.

The institutions of the City grew progressively stronger, for solid foundations had been laid in good time. Back in Elizabeth's reign Antwerp had lost its position as the principal trading and financial centre of northern Europe when it had been sacked by the Spaniards in 1585. A third of its most experienced traders moved straight across to London to operate in a Royal Exchange which Elizabeth had opened fourteen years earlier. This had been a gift to the City by Sir Thomas Gresham, a rich mercer who had been the royal agent in Antwerp between 1551 and 1567, and it was so closely modelled on the Antwerp exchange that the immigrant dealers must have found the new environment very familiar. Around the Royal Exchange a structured financial centre developed. The marine assurers moved into rooms in the building and operated there until it was destroyed in the Great Fire; then they found their way to a coffee-house in Lombard Street, kept by a man called Lloyd whose intelligence of vessels' movements was collected and published there. The coffee-houses were important meeting places. The North and South American Coffee-house, for example, had an elegantly-furnished subscription room behind its public quarters, where merchants were provided with detailed news of the arrival and departure of vessels at American ports, and bankers and the London heads of American and continental companies looked in regularly to keep in touch. Similarly, all the merchants and brokers engaged in the Russian trade in tallow, oil, hemp and seed met at the Baltic Coffee-house in Threadneedle Street, which had a public saleroom upstairs. As a symbolic, as well as very practical, ultimate expression of City strength, the Bank of England was established in 1694.

But the seventeenth century was not without its problems, and the biggest of them was the Dutch. They were building bigger ships, mounting more ambitious expeditions, driving harder bargains. They seemed to be everywhere, and by 1629 it had to be recognised that they were invincible at sea. They had poured money into a Dutch West India Company which had government support and its own fleet of warships, and which swept the Caribbean, seized vast amounts of booty from the Spaniards, and settled much of the coast of Brazil, as well as an area in the north which they called Nieu Amsterdam. In the Far East they had a firm hold on the East Indies trade; sometimes bargaining with the English, and sometimes massacring them, they had effectively contained them in their Indian Empire. When the English were preoccupied with their Civil War, the Dutch missed no chance to strengthen their hold on commerce. They paused on their voyages to the East to explore the Cape and by 1652 they had colonised South Africa. When the 1651 Navigation Act prohibited imports into England except in English-built vessels, the Dutch were furious and the bitter dispute which followed led to war between the two countries in 1652-4. The English captured or destroyed 700 Dutch merchant ships and England's trading position was restored. Competition continued unabated. The Dutch still dominated the Oriental trade, with a hundred vessels of about 600 tons sailing regularly between the Netherlands and the East Indies. In 1664 the English fleet seized Nieu Amsterdam and it was renamed New York; only after the deed was war declared again. The peace settlement of 1667 saw the Dutch finally expelled from North America, while the English withdrew from Surinam. There was war again in 1672-4, with England allied with France, which had by then built up a powerful navy. The English opted out in 1674, leaving the French and Dutch to fight on for four years more, while London concentrated on further development of its seaborne trade. By the end of the century, the Dutch had been dealt with and the new adversary was France, with whom the struggle was to continue until the Battle of Waterloo in 1815.

Among the earliest statistics of English trade are those quoted by Edward Missenden in 1623. He stated that between Christmas 1612 and Christmas 1613 English exports totalled £2,090,436 and imports £2,141,151, and he quoted figures for the Customs dues collected which indicate that about 70 per cent of exports and 78 per cent of imports passed through the Port of London. By 1623 exports had increased by about eleven per cent and imports by 21 per cent. The principal ports with which London traded at the time were Naples, Genoa, Leghorn, Marseilles, Malaga, Bordeaux, Middleburgh, Hamburg, Danzig, Newfoundland and Greenland.

The expansion and improvement of the port to handle the rapid increase in traffic came more by accident than by design. The merchants were diligent in protecting their rights and privileges, but less energetic in developing facilities. James the First, during his twenty-two years' reign, signed three charters reaffirming the rights of the City to measure and weigh cargoes and to charge for the service and for "bailiff and conservation of the water of Thames" from Staines Bridge to Yantlet Creek in the Medway. Charles the First later reaffirmed all these rights and ruled that the City should be responsible for packing and porterage of all goods in the port; he made a new grant of "scavage" — a right to survey goods belonging to aliens for the purpose of assessing Customs duties; and he decreed that anyone handling merchandise in the port must be a Freeman of the City. The merchants' rights were well safeguarded, but the Legal Quays were congested and the warehouses seriously inadequate.

Disasters came one upon another: first the plague in 1665, killing 100,000 people in London within six months; then the Great Fire in 1666, destroying virtually the whole of the port area — it began in Pudding Lane, an east wind blew the flames from warehouse to warehouse, with vast quantities of brandy, pitch, resin and sulphur fuelling the conflagration until finally nothing remained standing between the Tower and Temple Church; finally a blockade of the Thames by the Dutch which resulted in much damage and suffering.

Thus came an opportunity for a planned new start to fit the port for its tasks. The most ambitious of the new projects was for one long Thames Quay,

forty feet wide, running uninterrupted from Tower to Temple. It was to
replace the huddles of sheds, disordered yards and dilapidated equipment
which had occupied the area before the Fire. Unfortunately, there were delays
and, by the time the City was ready to proceed, the wharfingers had completed
their own reconstruction below London Bridge and the shipowners professed
themselves satisfied. The biggest improvement that materialised was a widening
of Thames Street to thirty feet and a levelling of the access lanes to the quays,
so that heavy carts could reach the waterfront. A second project was to dredge
the Fleet river so that craft drawing five feet of water might get up as far as
Holborn Bridge. This scheme was carried through; wharves 32 feet wide were
constructed on either side of the channel, with storage vaults beneath them
and warehouses behind. But, perversely, this improvement secured little
support from the merchants. Few chose to rent the new premises and the
wharves were used for everything except their intended purpose. As a result,
by 1733 the Fleet was covered over as far as Fleet bridge, and in 1766 the rest
of it disappeared underground in preparation for the erection, three years
later, of the second bridge over the Thames, at Blackfriars. At about this time,

Many early river quays such as this survived into the nineteenth century, when steamships arrived
to cast a pall over primitive machinery and congested berths.   *Courtesy P.L.A.*

important developments were taking place further down-river. The East India Company developed its facilities at Blackwall, where its vessels ended their voyages at mid-stream moorings and discharged into lighters. The Company constructed several dry docks, in which to build and repair its ships. The earliest reference to any sort of wet dock is in Samuel Pepys's diary; he records that on 15th January, 1661, he went to Blackwall to see a new merchantman, the *Royal Oak*, which was about to be launched, but also to view "the new wet dock". It was the first such, one and a half acres in area, intended for the fitting out of vessels after launching.

With the eighteenth century, reliable statistical information about shipping movements and about the trade handled in London is available for the first time. It demonstrates the dominant position of the port at that period. London handled 77 per cent by value of all foreign trade in 1700. Almost half the imports arrived in foreign vessels, and they carried about 38 per cent of exports. London, however, had 560 registered vessels, totalling 84,882 tons, with 10,065 men, while the next biggest port, Bristol, had only 165 vessels totalling 17,338 tons, with 2,359 men. Liverpool had 102 vessels, totalling 8,619 tons with 1,101 men, and was less important, in terms of number of registered vessels, than Yarmouth, Exeter, Hull and Whitby. The vessels in the overseas trade from and to the Thames were still not large: they averaged about 150 tons, but the majority of them were much smaller than that. In 1732 there were two vessels of 750 tons registered at London: the *Prince Frederick* and the *Prince William*, and one of 495 tons, the *Prince Augustus.* These were the largest, but there were about 200 others of more than 200 tons, and 1,202 of or under 200 tons.

As the century progressed, England steadily consolidated its world power and trade expanded rapidly, with exports moving to a spectacular crescendo during the last two decades. Marlborough's victories on the continent ruined French commerce; by the middle of the century Clive had smashed French power in India; by 1763 the last French Governor of Canada had surrendered and the whole of Canada passed to the British Crown. As with Spain and the Netherlands in earlier centuries, so now with France the score was settled in the trading outposts and the financial and commercial markets of the world. Trans-Atlantic trade developed fast, but so did the west coast ports of Liverpool, Glasgow and Bristol, and the emergence of the cotton mills of Lancashire and the hardware factories of the Midlands favoured these rival ports. London, however, held on to an impressive share, and did well as the West Indies trade expanded. About the middle of the century the Royal Africa Company and the Levant Company surrendered, in return for compensation, their exclusive privileges, with the result that trade with Africa and with the Middle East increased dramatically. Monopoly was shown to be a curb on commerce, but the East India Company held on to its privileges throughout this period and the explosion in exports to India and the Far East did not come until the nineteenth century.

By 1800 London handled a third of the trade of the Empire: something like £70 millions worth each year. Congestion and confusion in the river was appalling; not only were there the big merchantmen of the East India Company at Blackwall, the rather smaller West Indiamen of 350 to 500 tons discharging at Deptford, and the 300-ton vessels sailing to the Baltic, each of which discharged enough timber into the river to occupy twelve times the water surface required by the vessel itself. The vessels in the foreign trade were outnumbered four to one by coastal vessels, nearly 250 of them arriving in the river every week. Three-fifths of these were colliers from the north-east, and there were sometimes 300 of them in the river at the same time. They were serviced by well over 2,000 coal barges and half of these were, in effect, used for storage, merchants drawing off supplies as they required them. Apart from the coal barges, there were about 1,200 lighters, hoys and other similar craft at work each day. Each of the lighters was propelled by a single oar, or sweep, and each carried up to 100 tons from vessels moored in mid-stream to the wharves, or from wharf to wharf in different parts of the port. There were increasing numbers of Thames barges, which each carried up to 400 tons beneath a big mainsail and a small mizzen. The watermen still operated about 3,000 wherries for passengers.

In the midst of this maelstrom of activity on the river, a significant fishing industry still existed, a great part of the fleet based in the two-mile Roding creek up to the Essex village of Barking. Information about fishing in 1768 was provided by Mr Goldham, the Clerk of Billingsgate Market. He recalled that there had been 400 Thames fishermen, each owning his own boat and employing a boy. They fished between London and Deptford and made a reasonable living catching roach, plaice, smelt, flounders, salmon, shad, eels, gudgeon, dace and dabs. Fifty thousand smelt were brought daily to Billingsgate and not fewer than 3,000 Thames salmon in a season. As late as 1810, Mr Goldham added, ten salmon and 3,000 smelt had been taken at one haul near Wandsworth. But by 1828, when the Parliamentary Committee was hearing this evidence, the Thames fishery had been almost destroyed, though Billingsgate remained for long after that a busy fish market to which vessels from Faversham, Maldon, Rochester, Colchester and Dover brought their catches daily. They arrived at evening or during the night and moored beside each other on either side of a floating platform, from which steps ascended to the open fish market on the quay.

There was no organised system for mooring ships in the river; each master tied up wherever he could find a vacant berth. There is a record of there having been 775 vessels in the Upper Pool at moorings designed for 545.

The Upper Pool 1804. This engraving by William Daniell, R.A. shows the congestion caused by vessels tied up at moorings in the river.   *Courtesy P.L.A.*

Sometimes vessels waited a week before they could even enter the Pool, and then were held for three to four weeks before discharge was completed.

The West Indian merchants were the first to become militant, for the seasonal pattern and the high value of their shipments accentuated their problems. Sugar was cropped from January to July and arrived in London during a few summer months, so that as many as 35,000 to 40,000 hogsheads could arrive in a single convoy. As available warehouses could only hold 32,000, sugar was often piled six or eight hogsheads high on the quayside. In the second half of the eighteenth century imports of sugar and rum from the West Indies increased four-fold and by 1792 London's predominant share of this trade involved 285 ships carrying 105,000 hogsheads. The merchants concerned demanded a complete reorganisation of the port. They pointed out that London only had 1,400 lineal feet of quays, whereas Bristol had expanded to 4,000 feet. They accused the wharfingers who owned the Legal Quays of combining into a monopoly which had forced up rates. London was in danger of losing business to other ports. Parliament half-heartedly promised an enquiry, but no effective action followed.

The only ameliorative move was the creation of new "sufferance wharves" on the south bank, where Customs officers attended as necessary to supervise landings of certain specified goods. By 1796 the Legal Quays plus the sufferance wharves lined almost the whole of the banks of the Upper Pool, from London Bridge to Hermitage Stairs on the north side and to St Saviour's Dock on the south. The accommodation, however, remained quite inadequate, and the grievances of the shipowners and merchants actually increased, for the owners of the sufferance wharves were admitted into the monopoly of the north bank owners and charges were not reduced. The City Corporation, as the port authority, tried to evade responsibility; when compelled to take a stand, it sided with the monopolists.

By the turn of the century, conditions amounted to a scandal. The accident rate was dreadful: five hundred people were drowned in the Pool of London in a single year. Inadequate attention had been paid to maintaining sufficient depth of water for shipping, as the rapidly-growing city dumped its sewage thoughtlessly into the stream, ballast was freely spilled over ships' sides, and natural siltage occurred. The average tide in 1800 provided more than 20 feet of water for more than three hours in any part of the channel up to London Bridge, but at many of the wharves the depth of water available was reduced by four or five feet during the course of the eighteenth century.

All this was bad for business, but what was worse was the organised theft and plunder. Many cargoes which had to be left in stacks on the wharves, with insufficient protection, were not only valuable in themselves, but were subject to heavy taxation. Apart from wines and spirits, London had become the principal entrepôt for the Continent for tobacco shipments from America. Organised gangs went into action at dusk and there was almost as much activity on the river by night as by day. It was estimated that 11,000 people made a dishonest living on the proceeds. Different groups of workers operated together during these night exploits; the watermen emerged as the "Night Plunderers", the porters and labourers as the "Heavy Horsemen", the ships' mates and revenue-men as the "Light Horsemen". There were "River Pirates", who used pickaxes and choppers. There were "Mudlarks" and "Scuffle-Hunters" and "Peterboatmen", all with their specialities in crime. It was difficult to know where it all began and ended. Not only Customs officers, but some of the City merchants themselves, were suspected of complicity. Patrick Colquhoun, a Metropolitan magistrate and part-founder of the first Thames Marine Police Force, estimated that 0.84 per cent by value of the trade of the port was lost by plunder, and as much as two per cent of the West Indies trade. Other estimates range between £500,000 and £800,000-worth of goods stolen every year throughout the final decade of the century. When the merchants eventually created a private Marine Police Force it found itself fighting pitched battles, in which several officers were killed, but £100,000-worth of stolen goods were recovered in its first year of operation.

Developments which had meanwhile taken place down-river had a significance for the future which no-one at first foresaw. The first wet dock, which the East India Company had constructed at Blackwall for the fitting out of vessels, was followed in 1700 by a similar, but much larger, wet dock on the south side of the river. Until that year, London on the south bank did not extend east of Southwark; Bermondsey was an island in a marsh, beyond it the open fields. There a private developer constructed what was called the Howland Great Wet Dock, 1,070 feet long by 500 feet wide, with an area of over ten acres. For more than a century this remained the largest dock in the port, able to accommodate the largest merchant ships of the time. No warehouses were provided, however, and this fact, coupled with the provision of a crane for masting and dismasting and the position close to the naval shipyard at Deptford, suggests that the Howland Dock was originally intended for ship repair, rather than for trade. In 1763, however, it was adapted for the whaling fleet, which by then was sailing from London to northern waters; the name was changed to the Greenland Dock and facilities were installed to extract oil from blubber. This was a prosperous trade for about half a century and at its peak it engaged 255 vessels. When the dock changed hands again, however, in 1806, whaling was in decline and so it became an entrepôt for timber and corn and its name was changed to the Commercial Dock; but this anticipates developments described in the following chapter.

The sponsors of the Howland Dock made great play of the relative safety of vessels berthed there when weather was bad, and there were also security advantages which became increasingly obvious as time passed. By 1789 the East India Company began to think about an expansion of its docks at Blackwall, possibly with a dawning understanding that the Greenland Dock was a symbol of what was to come, and in the following year it extended its existing enclosed basin to form a new Brunswick Dock. Cranes were provided to handle heavy stores and guns, but there was no commitment to the use of the dock for cargo handling.

As the eighteenth century closed London was still a river port, with old London Bridge at its heart. The bridge prevented passage of all but the smallest vessels, and even these were restricted to short periods before and after high water. Various efforts were made to improve matters: in 1759 one large arch was created in place of the two middle arches; in 1761 all the houses on the bridge were removed, so that the roadway could be widened to 31 feet; between 1756 and 1798 the sum of £78,835 was spent on bridge repairs. All this was mere tinkering, and finally it was recognised that a new bridge must be built. It was positioned 100 feet upstream of the earlier crossing and it was opened by King William IV in 1831. By that time the whole aspect of the Port of London had been dramatically transformed.

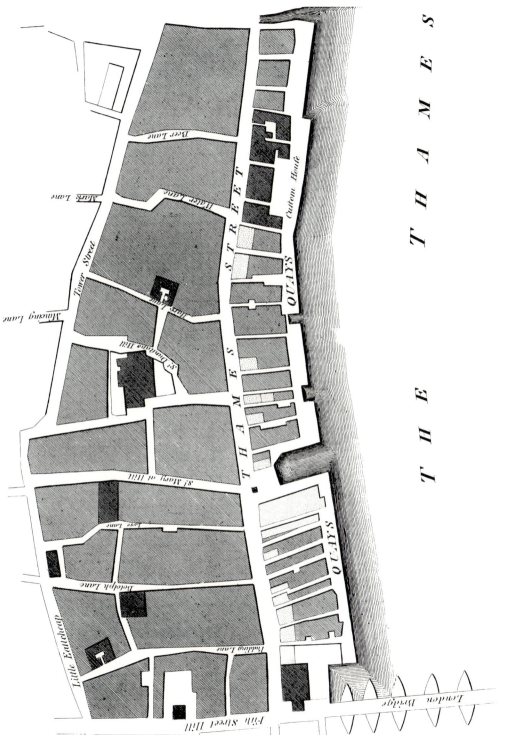

The Legal Quays 1796. From the time of Queen Elizabeth I until the construction of the enclosed docks in the early nineteenth century, most of the trade of the port passed over the 1,464 feet of riverside quays between London Bridge and the Tower of London. The largest of the docks is Billingsgate.

Courtesy P.L.A.

George Hibbert, the first chairman of the first dock company, formed in 1799 to construct the West India Docks. Oil painting by Sir Thomas Lawrence, P.R.A.
Courtesy P.L.A.

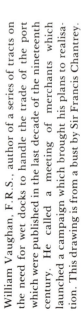

William Vaughan, F.R.S., author of a series of tracts on the need for wet docks to handle the trade of the port which were published in the last decade of the nineteenth century. He called a meeting of merchants which launched a campaign which brought his plans to realisation. This drawing is from a bust by Sir Francis Chantrey.
Courtesy P.L.A.

CHAPTER FOUR

The Enclosed Docks

A S CONGESTION and crime brought the Port of London to the edge of chaos in the closing years of the eighteenth century, the West Indian merchants launched a vigorous agitation for improvement of facilities and organisation. The campaign was led by a man of exceptional imagination, energy and determination, William Vaughan. He had very special qualifications for his role. His father was a London merchant and his mother came from Massachusetts. It was understood from his schooldays that he would follow a mercantile career, and he wrote of them: "My studies were much directed to geography, history, travel and voyages of discovery. I took great interest in accounts of shipwrecks and other disasters at sea . . .". One of his teachers was the scientist, Dr Joseph Priestley, and afterwards Vaughan worked for a time in the Greenland dock. When he was only thirty-one he was elected a director of the Royal Exchange Assurance Corporation and later he was appointed its Governor. He became a Fellow of the Royal Society.

It was Vaughan who produced the first constructive proposals for the provision of enclosed docks and who brought into existence an effective pressure group. In 1793 he published a tract — the first of a series — titled: "On Wet Docks, Quays and Warehouses for the Port of London, with hints respecting Trade". It proposed the construction of enclosed docks on three separate sites: St Katharine's, Wapping; the Isle of Dogs; and Rotherhithe. Within thirty years, this programme had been completely fulfilled. Vaughan convened a meeting of chairmen of public bodies and of merchant companies to consider the state of the Legal Quays; it took place at the Merchant Seamen's Office on 6th March, 1794, and appointed a committee which, exactly one year later, recommended that "wet docks at Wapping would best tend to remove the difficulties and inconveniences which affect the commerce of the Port".

A subscription was opened and a petition presented to Parliament, after which the Commons set up its own Committee under Sir William Young and with the Prime Minister, William Pitt, as a member. This Committee heard the evidence of 59 witnesses during 1796 and the conditions of confusion which have already been described were fully explained to it. It was established that there had been as many as 1,300 ships, quite apart from the 3,000 small wherries still operating, packed into the river port on a single day. Now it was proposed that the great majority of these vessels should be swept from the river into enclosed docks constructed on either side of it. There was plenty of undeveloped land, though one of Vaughan's proposed sites, at Wapping, was covered with the squalid homes of a community of three thousand immigrants from France and the Low Countries, who lived beside the Hospital of St Katharine, a religious foundation which dated back to Queen Matilda in 1148. Down stream, however, the Isle of Dogs was empty marshland, nine windmills dotting its western embankment. Beyond that, the East India Company was well established and had just recently expanded its facilities. Further out still, there were villages at Poplar, Bow and Bromley, but the Lea Marshes had prevented any large-scale development. South of the river little had been built between Southwark, at the southern end of London Bridge, and the Greenland Dock; Bermondsey was unclaimed marshland. Further down, there were the dockyards at Deptford and Woolwich.

Eight possible alternative schemes for wet docks were placed before the Commons Committee. Established vested interests in the port and the City manoeuvred to retain their privileges; wharfingers, watermen, lightermen and the City Corporation presented every kind of objection to enclosed docks. Their combined arguments failed to dent the case of Vaughan and his supporters and the Committee recommended the construction of docks, but left Parliament to make a choice between the various projects. Once the Committee's report was out, there was a rush to prepare and to bring before Parliament suitable legislation, each private bill being presented by a company formed for the purpose. A whole catalogue of docks projects was quickly created, covering both banks of the river. The West India Dock Company, which held its first statutory meeting on 8th August, 1799, was first off the mark and secured an Act in that same year authorising it to enclose 295 acres in the Isle of Dogs, between Limehouse and Blackwall, and to construct an enclosed dock there. In the following year a London Dock Company received Parliamentary approval for a dock at Wapping, and in 1803 another Act authorised construction of enlarged East India Docks.

The activities of each of these early companies followed very much the same pattern and the story of the early years of the West India Dock concern is representative. Once an Act of Parliament had been secured, optimism was unbridled and planning proceeded on the most ambitious scale. The inaugural meeting of the Company took place at the London Tavern, in Bishopsgate, and this was to be the scene of many such meetings and of the junketing which accompanied stone-laying and official opening ceremonies in later years. The London Tavern had been opened about thirty years before, was a favourite resort of merchants and shippers, and had developed a particularly close association with the East India Company. It was a large and opulent establishment, its biggest dining room able to seat over 350 for dinner, its

In 1831 a new London Bridge replaced the one which had stood for centuries and which had been the heart of the Port of London. The buildings on the ancient bridge had been cleared 75 years earlier. The new bridge was built upstream of the old one, and this water-colour by G. B. Moore was made while they still stood side-by-side.

Courtesy P.L.A.

wines and its food, particularly its turtle soup, the talk of the town. Practically all the merchants trading to the West Indies gathered there in August 1799 and pledged their support to the new enterprise. A total of 123 shareholders subscribed an initial capital of £500,000, and later on this was increased to £1,200,000. A natural choice as the first chairman of the company was George Hibbert, who had been a pioneer campaigner alongside William Vaughan. Hibbert's father had traded with the West Indies and the son had succeeded to the business and had become the chairman of the West Indies merchants, as well as Agent for Jamaica. He was also a wharfinger in the Port and a City Alderman. A lucid and forcible speaker, he now emerged as the most powerful influence on docks development.

The foundation stone of the West India Docks was laid on 12th July, 1800 — the first anniversary of the Royal Assent to the Act of Parliament. Elaborate ceremony and a general air of holiday marked the occasion, and the guests included the Prime Minister (William Pitt), the Lord Chancellor, the First Lord of the Admiralty, several other Ministers and the President of the Royal Society. A glass bottle placed inside the foundation stone contained a statement in Latin of the Company's intention that the docks should be: "For the Distinct Purpose of complete security and ample accommodation (Hitherto not afforded) To the shipping and produce of the West Indies at this wealthy Port . . . An undertaking which, under the Favour of God, shall contribute Stability, Increase and Ornament to British Commerce". After the stone-laying there was "an elegant entertainment" at the London Tavern, the language becoming more flowery as the day progressed. After toasts to the King and the Constitution, the next one was: "Success to the works at the Isle of Dogs, and may our cornerstone stand firm under the weight of increasing commerce." Then followed toasts to the City of London (which was to get a ship canal across the Isle of Dogs from Blackwall to Limehouse as part of the overall scheme); to the West Indian Colonies; to the Parliamentarians and the City Fathers; and finally a toast which introduced the only ambivalent note: "Peace with security and honour, or war with unanimity and vigour" — a reference to the war with France which was not going too well at that time.

The West India Dock was handsomely, indeed lavishly, designed and constructed. There were two parallel basins, each half a mile long; a 500-feet-wide Import Dock to the north of the site and a 400-feet-wide Export Dock beside it. A depth of 31 feet of water was provided, which was sufficient to take any vessel able to come so far up the river. A lock at the Blackwall (eastern) end was used by vessels arriving and leaving, and a lock at the Limehouse (western) end was used by lighters transferring the cargoes up-river: a business-like arrangement to reduce congestion. The Import Dock was carefully laid out to deal efficiently with its special needs. On its north quay the architect George Gwilt and his son raised nine Georgian warehouses, most of them of five storeys, totalling 2,800 feet in length: the largest continuous frontage of any buildings in Europe. Only three had been completed when the Dock was officially opened, but the others followed soon afterwards. These warehouses were used mainly for the storage of sugar and molasses — the principal product of the West Indies — and they could hold the port's entire annual import. On the opposite side of the dock, on the south quay, there were storage sheds and open ground for timber, with vaults beneath for the storage of rum, the other major Caribbean import. The Export Dock had few buildings, but was well equipped with cranes for loading cargoes; these cranes were operated solely by man-power, usually applied at winches, but also by gangs marching inside large wooden drums, using the principle of the treadmill.

Much attention was paid to security; the West Indian merchants intended that pilferage of their cargoes should be stopped once and for all time. The Act of Parliament laid down that the docks should be protected by 30 feet walls of brick or stone, supplemented by a ditch twelve feet wide and six feet deep, and that no buildings should stand within one hundred yards of the exterior face of the walls. These requirements were later modified, so that 20

The Royal Naval College at Greenwich. *Photograph by Douglas Brown*

feet walls only were provided, at the east and west ends of the docks, but these were still grimly formidable. By way of relief, an ornate Clock Gate surmounted by a ship carved in stone, about six feet high, was erected to commemorate the work of construction. It was demolished in 1832 and the ship was removed to Poplar Recreation Ground, but has since disappeared.

Just inside this entrance gate two guardhouses were provided for small detachments of troops which the government made available during the early years after the docks were opened. They provided a cordon of eight sentries around the whole area and in each sentry-box there was a bell which was sounded at regular intervals so long as all was well. At various strategic points 18-pounder guns were placed. As a final mark of government approval of mercantile enterprise, the Prime Minister, Henry Addington (later Lord Sidmouth), went down to the East End on 27th August, 1802, to board a newly-built small West Indiaman named after him which, decorated with the flags of all nations, then sailed into the dock to signify its completion. Behind it followed the first cargo-carrying vessel, the *Echo*, with 800 to 900 hogsheads of sugar. The dock opened for normal business five days later.

During the eighteenth century, as the produce of Britain's first colonies was compulsorily carried to London, much of it for subsequent re-export, the Customs gave concessions to the merchants in order to assist them to fulfil their entrepôt role. From 1714 tobacco importers were required to deposit only a small portion of the import duty when a cargo arrived, and this sum was refunded if the cargo was subsequently exported. In 1742 similar arrangements were made so that rum could be warehoused in London for months without payment of duty, and similar treatment was extended to rice in 1765 and to coffee in 1767. With the opening of the first of the enclosed docks a formal system of bonded warehouses was instituted. All the quays and wharfs within the dock walls were regarded as "legal quays" and the gates and doors of the premises were placed under joint locks of Company and Inland Revenue. Duty was payable only when goods were withdrawn from the warehouses. In 1803 a Warehousing Act consolidated the system, provided for its extension into other new docks as they were completed, and so opened the way for unlimited expansion for entrepôt trade. When ships arrived at Gravesend their hatches were fastened down and locked and sealed by Customs officers, and they could not be opened again until the vessels were in dock. These arrangements also served to safeguard cargoes against theft; in this respect, the Dock Company took other stringent measures to supplement them. It employed its own labourers, who were searched as they left the docks each day, and no outside porters or carmen were permitted on to the quays. A Company police force was created. The Company later claimed that as a result of its security measures over the first twenty years merchants benefitted to the tune of over £5 millions and the Revenue by almost £3,400,000. Expressed in another way, it meant that the amount of rum which inexplicably disappeared was reduced from four gallons per case in the old days of river discharge to about four table-spoonfuls per case in the docks.

The West India Docks Act, and several of the most important similar Acts which followed, contained two important provisions which had immense long-term significance for the whole Port of London. The first of these bestowed monopoly privileges on the Company; for twenty-one years from the completion of the docks all vessels arriving from any West Indian port with West Indian products was obliged to land cargoes within the West India Docks. Only tobacco was excluded; it had to be taken to a King's Tobacco Warehouse elsewhere on the river. Ships carrying West Indian products but arriving from other ports were required to discharge in the docks if the Commissioners of Customs so decided. Similar rules applied to ships and cargoes outward bound to the West Indies. The penalty if the law was broken was severe; the vessel could be forfeited, in addition to a heavy fine.

The dock companies found this monopoly highly beneficial. From 1803 onward the West India Company paid its shareholders a regular ten per cent dividend each year — after spending an estimated £600,000 out of revenue during the first twenty years on new capital works and placing additional large sums to reserve. Revenue was secured from charges levied on vessels docking and also on the cargoes they carried. The original scale of charges in the West India Docks secured 6s. 8d. per ton from vessels entering, to cover the costs of discharge, cooperage, hoops and nails as required for the handling of cargoes, and the right to load outward cargoes. Vessels had a right to remain in dock for up to six months. A few examples of the charges levied on cargoes landed are eightpence per hundredweight for sugar, one penny per gallon for rum, 1s. 6d. per hundredweight for cocoa or coffee, and 3s. 3d. per hundredweight for ginger.

The second clause in the early docks Acts which proved to be of crucial importance contained only 59 words, but they had a decisive effect on the development of the Port of London for a century and a half afterwards. This was the so-called "free water clause" which exempted from dock charges the lighters into which many vessels discharged their cargoes, even in the new docks. The clause stated: "Provided always and be it enacted that this Act shall not extend to charge with the said rate of duty of 6s. 8d. hereinbefore granted any lighters or craft entering into the said docks or basins or cuts to convey, deliver, discharge or receive ballast or goods to or from on board of any ship or ships, vessel or vessels." A time was to come when the dock companies, which started so bravely, were to lose their monopoly privileges, were to enjoy few Customs privileges not available equally to riverside wharves, and were to find that a high proportion of the cargoes brought through their locks into their dock basins were being discharged into lighters which then carried them

Brunswick Dock 1803. Built by John Perry for vessels of the East India Company, this dock at Blackwall was completed in 1790. The 120-foot high building for masting and dismantling ships is prominent in this oil painting by William Daniell, R.A.

Courtesy Trustees of the National Maritime Museum

away to be landed elsewhere. By 1850 over 50,000 barges a year were going into the West India Docks alone, averaging 30 tons each of carrying capacity. By the closing years of the nineteenth century dock companies were protesting that the "free water clause" was bankrupting them. Undeniably, the scale of lighterage activity was to become "the predominant characteristic in the functioning of the port".*

As the nineteenth century opened, however, all was optimism and enthusiasm. Hard on the heels of the West Indiamen, another group of merchants, most of them engaged in the wine and tobacco trade, established the London Dock Company to build a dock at Wapping; William Vaughan was among them. Their Act received the Royal Assent in June 1800; they retained as engineer the man who also built Dartmoor Prison, Daniel Alexander; the foundation stone was laid in June 1802; and the first vessel entered the new dock on 31st January, 1805. There were unexpected problems during construction; a great deal of housing property had to be purchased and demolished, and there were delays which proved expensive. But the original capital of £1,200,000 was topped up a number of times; a dock of twenty acres, with a basin and river lock and with warehouses to hold 24,000 hogsheads of tobacco, was completed; the Company enjoyed its monopoly for twenty-one years of all cargoes of tobacco, rice, wine and brandy, except for those from or to the East and West Indies; and the Prime Minister again appeared at the celebrations. All looked promising.

*Rodwell Jones, *Geography of London River* 1931.

The East India Company, having extended its dock at Blackwall in 1789-90, was already relatively well organised to control its cargoes when they reached London, and already it had enjoyed a monopoly of trade with the East for almost two hundred years. Its vessels anchored in the deep river water at Blackwall, their cargoes were lightered ashore and were then carried in a fleet of sixty four-wheeled covered wagons along the narrow, congested Ratcliffe Highway to warehouses in the City of London. These warehouses had only recently been built and were of a very high standard: Cutler Street and New Street, Bishopsgate, both opened in 1782, and Crutched Friars, built on a site purchased from the Crown in 1788 on which the Navy Office had stood in Pepys's time, and on which the P.L.A.'s first headquarters were to be built many years later. The Company's facilities at Blackwall were equally impressive; apart from its river moorings and wharf close by, there was the enlarged Brunswick Dock which, although still largely used for the fitting out and repair of the Company's vessels, could offer facilities for loading and discharge in special circumstances. Immediately adjoining was the private shipyard, P. Perry and Company, in which most of the East Indiamen were built.

As the general campaign for enclosed docks developed towards the turn of the century, the East India Company felt it necessary to re-examine its policy

Congestion in the River. Though this painting includes an early steamer, it conveys a vivid impression of the congestion in the port which characterised the late eighteenth century, before the docks were opened. *Courtesy P.L.A.*

West India Docks and City Canal. An engraving by William Daniell, R.A., made during the construction of the docks in 1802, showing the river frontage, the entrance locks, the Export and Import Docks with their great warehouses, and the City Canal to the south, cutting across the Isle of Dogs.   *Courtesy P.L.A.*

and needs. It joined the rush for a Parliamentary Act and its measure received Royal Assent in 1803; improvement and extension of the Blackwall complex began immediately and was completed in time for an official opening on 4th August, 1806. The Act created a subsidiary company, the East India Dock Company, bestowed upon it the usual twenty-one years monopoly rights, and decreed that Eastern cargoes must not only be brought into the new docks but must also be stored in the Company's City warehouses. The existing Brunswick Dock was enlarged and an entirely new dock was constructed alongside it, each having its own entrance. A 120-feet tower which had been used for many years for masting and dismasting vessels was retained and it survived until 1862. When the work had been completed, the East India Docks covered eight acres and could accommodate up to sixty vessels. At the riverside wharf, known as Blackwall Pier and used by emigrants to the Colonies as well as by day trippers to Margate, a new Brunswick Hotel opened for business and soon became famous for its whitebait dinners. There was also a new toll road into London, to by-pass the squalid Ratcliffe Highway; this was the outcome of a separate enterprise, the Commercial Road Company, headed by George Hibbert.

The celebration of these achievements on opening day in 1806 matched the ceremonies arranged in earlier years by the promoters of the West India and London Docks, but this time there was a military flavour which reflected something of the East India Company's traditions. A Royal Salute was fired from six regimental guns of the Company's Volunteers. Then the Trinity

House yacht sailed into the dock, followed by an East Indiaman, *Admiral Gardner*, each dressed with the flags of all nations, but care being taken, as a contemporary account noted, to fly "the French under all". A report in *The Globe* described how, as the vessels passed into the dock, the *Admiral Gardner* "answered the salute of the Regimental Artillery by firing her minute guns, while the Company's band on her quarter-deck played 'Rule Britannia' with full chorus from the ladies and gentlemen who crowded her decks". Afterwards, there was the usual "elegant dinner" at the London Tavern.

Apart from the three major companies already mentioned, a few entrepreneurs of more limited resources constructed smaller docks or basins on the north bank. The principal one was the ten-acre Limehouse Dock, which led into a canal to Paddington, where it linked with the Grand Junction Canal to give access to the Midlands.

Speculators were also busily prospecting on the south side of the river. The Surrey Canal Company, formed in 1801, proposed a canal from Rotherhithe to Epsom, with lateral cuts to a number of towns within easy reach; the idea was to provide cheap transport for the produce of Surrey horticulturists to the London markets. In fact, this canal never got beyond Camberwell. By 1804 there was a new project to develop a docks system and the canal was widened at one point to provide three acres of enclosed water, which was named the Grand Surrey Basin. Ambitions seem to have been unrestrained, but achievements were not spectacular. In 1825 the company raised more capital and advanced the idea of a "Grand Ship Canal" from the Thames to Portsmouth: "a tidal canal, without locks and navigable by ships of the largest size". Needless to add, this proved to be mere day-dreaming.

A more substantial south bank enterprise was the Commercial Dock Company, formed at a meeting at the London Tavern in September 1807, to

Four different companies developed the docks system — and the associated Surrey Canal — on the south side of the river during the early years of the nineteenth century. This aquatint by William Daniell, R.A. shows the Commercial Dock Company development around the earlier Greenland Dock — the original Howland Great Dock of 1700.　　　　　　　*Courtesy P.L.A.*

purchase for £35,000 the existing Greenland Dock and the adjoining Norway Dock. The whaling trade had declined, but the Baltic trade in timber, hemp, flax, pitch and tar was expanding and the new company hoped to switch these cargoes from the river. About 800 timber boats arrived each year from Scandinavia and the Baltic and others had their eyes on this potentially lucrative business. A rival Baltic Dock Company planned to convert a 45 acre estate at Rotherhithe into timber ponds, and a third undertaking, the East Country Dock Company, constructed an enclosed basin south of the Greenland Dock. The Commercial Dock Company secured its Act of Parliament in 1810 and almost immediately absorbed the Baltic Dock Company, but The East Country Company maintained a separate identity until 1851, when it, too, was absorbed.

Neither the Commercial Dock Company nor the Surrey Canal Company secured the twenty-one-years monopoly privileges of the three major dock companies on the north bank. When the first of these ran out on 2nd September, 1823 and the West India Dock Company applied to Parliament for its renewal, not surprisingly the Commercial Dock Company offered strong resistance. More remarkably, the London Dock Company also opposed the application. Its own twenty-one-year monopoly still had three years to run, and it saw the prospect of making good use of that period! In June 1823, a Commons Committee came down against continuance of monopoly rights for anyone. It accepted that it would be fairer if all the monopolies were ended simultaneously, but it noted that the West India Dock Company had accumulated big reserve funds and it suggested that, if these were used to reduce charges, the Company should be able to hold its own during the transition to free competition.

From 1824 shipowners were free to load or discharge wherever there were suitable facilities and the Revenue approved the security arrangements. The wharfingers who had owned the old Legal Quays had been compensated by the government when the new enclosed docks took over their trade; they had claimed £2 millions and had settled for £419,199. Now some of them came aggressively back into business. Old riverside wharves which had become disused were reconstructed as warehouses, conveniently situated close to the central markets. An Act of 1832 gave the Commissioners of Customs discretion to grant bonding facilities to these warehouses. The new competition was accentuated by the opening of a new docks complex at the very gateway to the City. The St Katharine Dock Company, which received Parliamentary approval of its plans in 1825, laid its foundation stone in May 1827 and was operational by October 1828. The now-familiar routine of flag-flying and gun-firing marked its opening, but the glamour of these occasions was wearing off and few national figures graced the occasion.

The St Katharine Dock Company retained Thomas Telford, one of the greatest engineers of his day, and he built to a unique plan. The handsome warehouses of yellow brick had arched arcades at quay level, but the upper floors were built along the water-line; the idea was that goods would be swung from vessels directly on to the floors on which they were to be stored. Great emphasis was placed upon the convenience of having these fine, modern bonded warehouses within a few minutes of the City merchants' offices. The total area of the St Katharine complex was about 25 acres, incorporating a basin of one and a half acres and two docks of about four acres each.

Unforeseen problems arose before and during construction. There were public protests at the destruction of the Royal Hospital and Church of St Katharine, which had stood on the site for seven centuries, enjoying throughout that period the personal patronage of successive queens. Compensation had to be paid for that, but also for the many streets of filthy slums—over one thousand of them in huddles with names like Dark Entry, Cat's Hole and Pillory Lane—which had to be swept away. By the time the dock was in business there was doubt and dismay to be sniffed in the Thames air. The reality was that there were now too many docks and wharves for the available traffic. There were no more twenty-one-year monopolies, the wharfingers were staging a come-back, the lightermen had free entry to remove cargoes wherever it suited them. The dock companies began to trim their charges and to cut their profits; from this time, few of them ever paid a satisfactory

London Dock 1816. This aquatint of London Dock seen from the north, by D. Havell (after H. Haseler), shows the impressive warehouses which, throughout the history of this dock, were a unique feature of the port.　　　　*Courtesy Trustees of the Museum of London*

The *Sons of the Thames*, an early nineteenth-century paddle boat, may have been the first steam vessel to enter the Thames. *Courtesy P.L.A.*

dividend to shareholders. Even the prosperous West India Dock Company, which had regularly paid ten per cent, reduced its dividends to five per cent in 1832 and to four and a half per cent in 1837. In 1829 the City Corporation recognised the complete failure of the canal which it had insisted should be cut across the Isle of Dogs, as part of its bargain with the West India Dock Company. The Company took it over, paying considerably less than its original cost, and it was widened into a new South Dock in which timber boats floated their cargoes. For a while the new St Katharine Dock Company did reasonably well, with a notably able chief executive, John Hall, whose vigorous management took much trade from the neighbouring London Docks.

The East India Company had special problems of its own. The India Bill of 1784 had removed from it political, financial and military control of the Indian Empire, which had been transferred into the hands of the British Government. When the Company's Charter came under the consideration of Parliament nine years later, concern was shown at the failure to build up any export trade to the Far East. The Company insisted that there was no worth-while market; the Commons, unconvinced, enacted that the Company should set aside 3,000 tons of its shipping each year for the use of private traders prepared to export. The East India Company's own employees made very good use of this facility, and many of them made fortunes by competing with the Company for its own trade in its own ships.

The year 1795 provided a dramatic proof of the Company's incompetence, or lack of will. A sharp increase in the price of corn in England had caused great distress and the East India management saw a prospect of handsome profits if it could import a large quantity of rice from India. In order to carry the maximum amount in the shortest time, it chartered many of the

Indian-built teak vessels which, until then, it had resolutely refused to admit to the regular trade. In order to get the most favourable charter rates from their owners, it agreed that they might carry return cargoes for their own exclusive benefit. Indian vessels sailed into the Thames for the first time, but by the time they arrived corn prices had fallen and rice proved not to be a very marketable commodity. The owners of the Indian ships, however, then loaded with French wines, cutlery, glassware of all kinds, cotton, silk and linen, and iron, lead tin and copper, scarcely any of which had ever been carried by the East India Company. These goods sold well, the shipowners made fantastic profits, and their success stimulated the efforts of other freelance importers. In 1814 an Act of Parliament opened trade to India to all comers and the result is shown by these statistics:

	1814	1817	1828
Indian Imports by East India Company	£826,558	£638,382	£488,601
Indian Imports by private traders	£1,048,132	£2,750,333	£3,979,072

After 1827 when the East India Dock Company lost its monopoly, the increasing trade was no longer obliged to go through its docks. In 1836 the parent company sold its City warehouses, "on giving up their trading associations"; in July 1838 the East and West India Dock Companies formally amalgamated; and in 1859 the original East India Company ceased to exist.

By the 1830s the initial impetus to provide docks in place of river wharves and moorings had run out. In the thirty-five years between publication of William Vaughan's first tract proposing wet docks and the opening of St Katharine Dock foreign imports, by tonnage, had increased by fifty per cent. In 1830 most of these increased imports were going into the new docks: nearly 870,000 tons, of a total of just over 950,000 tons. Nevertheless, congestion and confusion in the river had again become a serious problem, because of entirely new factors, and the City Corporation again found itself under pressure to solve the problems, or to reduce port dues.

One new factor, which operated on the port in two distinct ways, was Watt's discovery of the steam engine in 1784 and the subsequent expansion of the British coal-mining industry, particularly after the miner's safety-lamp came into use from 1815. Vastly increased quantities of coal were shipped to London from the north-east for the new machines and to meet the mounting domestic demand. The enlarged fleet of sail colliers mainly accounted for the increase in the number of vessels moored in the Thames from 8,001 in 1808 to 15,913 in 1824. By 1832 the quantity of coal shipped to London reached 2,139,078 tons in a single year. The other consequence of steam-power which added to river congestion was the appearance of the steamship. The first steamer on the Thames was the *Marjory* in 1814 and the first large iron steamship the *Rainbow* in 1838, trading between London, Ramsgate and Antwerp. The first Atlantic crossing by steam was in 1827, and the next one in 1828, when the *Royal William* (built in Canada for Samuel Cunard) crossed from Quebec to London in seventeen days. The new propulsion was to mean, in due time, a big change in port operation, for steam vessels could come up the river to the Pool on a single tide. But, initially, the effect of steam was to disorganise river activity.

The new vessels were enthusiastically received by a group of companies formed to operate passenger services. By 1835 eight companies were in keen competition. Between them, they had 33 steamers. They were:

The Gravesend Steam Packet Company, with eight vessels, calling at Gravesend, Southend and Sheerness (734 voyages).

The Diamond Steam Packet Company, with seven vessels, calling at Gravesend (2,280 voyages).

The Commercial Steam Packet Company, with six vessels, calling at Ramsgate, Southend and Sheerness (250 voyages).

The Woolwich Steam Packet Company, with three vessels, calling at Woolwich (five times daily in summer, twice daily in winter).

The General Steam Navigation Company, with three vessels, calling at Margate and Ramsgate (135 voyages).

The Margate and London New Steam Packet Company, with two vessels, calling at Margate (118 voyages).

The Herne Bay Company, with two vessels, calling at Herne Bay (179 voyages).

The Greenwich Steam Packet Company, with two vessels, calling at Greenwich (daily service).

The recently-in-business St Katharine Dock Company provided a wharf with 170 feet of river frontage to accommodate the new steamers, and another landing stage was provided near London Bridge. Captains employed by rival companies raced their vessels down the river without too much regard for the safety of other shipping, their more adventurous passengers often cheering them on. Outraged lightermen and boatmen sometimes lay on their oars and refused to move out of the fairway. Accidents were frequent. The City Corporation, as Conservators of the river, made regulations that steamships should not exceed three knots when travelling with the tide, or four knots against it, between London Bridge and the West India Docks, but these regulations were never enforced. The Watermen's Company tried to operate its bye-law limiting speed to five miles per hour, but the steamer captains insisted that it did not apply to them. The City Corporation tried again, with an injunction requiring that "a clear passage through the Pools should be kept of a width of not less than 300 feet"; again it was not enforced. In fact, travel by steamer was no quicker than by the coaches which ran from London to Gravesend in two and three-quarters hours, but it was more comfortable, and certainly more exciting. It was estimated that well over one million passengers passed Blackwall on board the steamers each year and that two-thirds of them embarked or disembarked at Gravesend. New life throbbed into that dying community, which had been by-passed by the movement of shipping into the new docks, by the disappearance of the fishing fleets, and by developing road traffic.

The shipowners and the London merchants, however, were now in revolt. In 1836 Sir John Hall, of St Katharine Dock, collected 5,700 signatures, including those of many of the most influential men in the City, petitioning Parliament for an enquiry into river navigation and congestion in the Pool. The Select Committee which was set up called for a unified control of the river and recommended that the government should bring in a bill in the session of 1837 to improve the regulation of the port. Much wrangling followed and it was not until 1857 that an Act was passed constituting the Thames Conservancy Board to take over the functions of the Navigation Committee of the City of London.

This aquatint by J. Phelps (after W. Ranwell) shows work in progress in January 1828 on the construction of the St Katharine Dock. It was opened later in the same year.

Courtesy P.L.A.

The *Elizabeth* entering St Katharine Dock on the opening day, 25th October, 1828 — an oil painting by William John Huggins.   *Courtesy P.L.A.*

By that time some of the problems had been eased as a result of the construction of railways. Increasingly, from 1845, much of London's coal arrived by rail, though a great deal continued to come by collier for the remainder of the century. In 1846, soon after the West India and East India Dock Companies had amalgamated, they joined with the Birmingham Junction Railway to establish a rail link to Chalk Farm (later the North London Railway), and so to the Midlands. The lines which opened at about the same time to Southend on the north bank and to Gravesend and Rochester in Kent quickly took most of the passengers from the steamers and most of the steamship companies collapsed. As the railways reached Dover, Folkestone and Newhaven the shorter sea crossings to the Continent drew away custom from those services which had sailed from the Thames to Ostend, Antwerp and Rotterdam. By 1860 the only such regular service which survived was to Hamburg, and it only remained in business by slashing its fares.

As Britain's industrial revolution gathered pace, with coal output leaping up year by year and far outstripping that of all the mines of all other countries combined, with Lancashire looms producing cotton manufactures in an ever-increasing flood, and with Midland factories getting fully into their stride, the commercial interests were avid for ever-widening markets. Most of the national revenue had hitherto been raised by Customs and Excise dues and the severe protectionist policies had been underwritten by Navigation Laws which for nearly two centuries had ensured that cargoes were carried in British ships. From 1820, when they first petitioned Parliament on the matter, London merchants were converted to a policy of free trade, and by the middle years of the century that policy had triumphed spectacularly. In his budget of 1842 Peel began to dismantle the elaborate system of tariffs, and he introduced income tax at sevenpence in the pound as an alternative source of national revenue. By 1860 the number of goods on which duty was levied had fallen from 1,052 to 48. In 1849 the Navigation Acts were repealed; British shipbuilders and shipowners no longer needed protection; their supremacy was such that eleven years later not a single foreign steamship had entered any of the colonial or coastal trades of London, and only about a fifth of foreign trade into the port was carried under foreign flags.

After the Hungry Forties there followed boom on an unprecedented scale; this was the age when Britain was, quite literally, the workshop of the world. When Peel presented his 1842 budget British exports totalled £47,250,000. By 1850 they were £71,367,000, by 1860 they were £135,842,000 and by 1870 their value soared to £200,000,000. London and its port enjoyed most of the benefit of this expansion of trade. We are fortunate to have a very detailed account of the activities of the port at the middle of the nineteenth century in a book published in 1862, "The Port and Trade of London", compiled by the then manager of the Victoria Docks, Charles Capper. Britain claimed 49 colonies at that time and her imports from them in 1860, by values, were as follows:

Australia	£21,982,286 (including gold)
Far East	£12,498,758
North America	£10,907,493
West Indies	5,788,803
Africa	2,629,439
Mediterranean and others	2,477,040
Total colonial imports	£56,283,819

Additionally, imports from the Indian Empire were valued at £15,106,595. The declared value of British products and manufactures exported to the colonies in 1860 was £26,699,543 and to the Indian Empire it was £17,683,669. Thus, the total value of Britain's trade with her overseas possessions was something like £115,000,000, which was a little less than a third of her total overseas trade.

London had a virtual monopoly of the trade with India and most of the Far East. Of 702 vessels, totalling 530,378 tons, entered inwards in 1860 from the East Indies and Singapore, 634 totalling 437,034 tons, came to London, leaving only 68 ships between all other U.K. ports.

London enjoyed over half of the trade with the West Indies and Caribbean, with 471 vessels, totalling 143,325 tons, out of a total of 814 vessels, totalling 250,486 tons. Britain's single most important trading partner was the United States, which in 1860 took nearly £23 millions of British exports and sent nearly £45 millions of British imports. In the days before steam London had enjoyed a good part of this traffic, with first-class passenger ships sailing from the Thames and calling at Southampton or Plymouth, but the development of the steamship and of the Lancashire cotton industry switched most of this trade to Liverpool. London merchants turned a part of their attention to South America and by 1860 they had secured about a third of the business, with 176 vessels of 62,181 tons coming to the Thames.

In Europe the principal trading partner was Russia, which supplied three-quarters of Britain's needs of tallow for use as lubricants and for candle and soap-making. Though our exports to Russia fell far short of these imports, there was promise of rapid expansion indicated by increases, over a three year period to 1860, from £175,000 to £630,000 in sales of iron, from £61,600 to £193,000 in sales of steam engines, and from £1,600 to £48,500 in sales of agricultural implements.

The great entrepôt of northern Europe was Hamburg, which did about £20 millions of trade a year with London. The Prussian ports of Stettin and

St Katharine's Dock House. A nineteenth-century sketch of the dock premises which stood nearest to, and directly faced, the City of London. This building was destroyed during the Second World War. The headquarters of the Port of London Authority moved to a building on the same site in 1972.   *Courtesy P.L.A.*

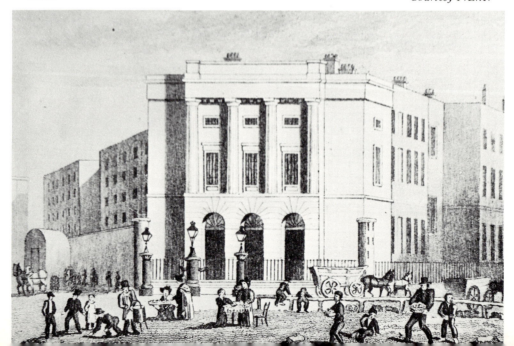

Danzig did about £10½ millions between them. The major British export was yarn and textiles, the principal import grain. Trade with the Mediterranean was shared with other U.K. ports, but London had 241 ships of 50,000 tons trading with Italy in 1860, it enjoyed a virtual monopoly of the dried fruit trade with Greece and the Ionian Islands, and it did good business with Constantinople, once again the entrepôt for the Middle East and Russia.

To round off this picture of the busy port of 1860, it must be noted that the coastal trade in that year involved 15,533 sailing vessels and 2,832 steamships inwards and 6,925 sailing vessels and 1,893 steamships cleared, with cargoes totalling about four and a quarter million tons.

Although the nature of port activity must be defined statistically, as Charles Capper did most conscientiously, the real flavour of the quayside can be conveyed only by an eye-witness with special descriptive powers. Fortunately, Henry Mayhew has left us such a description, of London Dock in about the year 1850:

"As you enter the dock the sight of the forest of masts in the distance, and the tall chimneys vomiting clouds of black smoke, and the many coloured flags flying in the air, has a most peculiar effect; while the sheds with their monster wheels arching through the roofs look like the paddle-boxes of huge steamers.

"Along the quay you see, now men with their faces blue with indigo, and now gaugers, with their long brass-tipped rules dripping with spirit from the cask they have been probing. Then will come a group of flaxen-haired sailors chattering German; and next a black sailor with a cotton handkerchief twisted turban-like round his head. Presently, a blue-smocked butcher, with fresh meat and a bunch of cabbages in the tray on his shoulder; and shortly afterwards a mate with green paroquets in a wooden cage.

"Here you will see sitting on a bench a sorrowful-looking woman, with new bright cooking-tins at her feet, telling you she is an emigrant preparing for her voyage.

"As you pass along this quay, the air is pungent with tobacco; on that, it overpowers you with the fumes of rum; then you are nearly sickened with the stench of hides and huge bins of horns; and shortly afterwards the atmosphere is fragrant with coffee and spice. Nearly everywhere you meet stacks of cork, or else yellow bins of sulphur or lead-coloured copper ore.

"As you enter this warehouse, the flooring is sticky, as if it had been newly tarred, with the sugar that has leaked through the casks; and as you descend into the dark vaults, you see long lines of lights hanging from the black arches, and lamps flitting about midway. Here you sniff the fumes of the wine, and there the peculiar fungus-smell of dry rot; then the jumble of sounds as you pass along the dock blends in anything but sweet concord.

"The sailors are singing boisterous nigger songs from the Yankee ship just entering; the cooper is hammering at the casks on the quay; the chains of the cranes, loosed of their weight, rattle as they fly up again; the ropes splash in the water; some captain shouts his orders through his hands; a goat bleats from some ship in the basin; and empty casks roll along the stones with a heavy drum-like sound.

"Here the heavily-laden ships are down far below the quay, and you descend to them by ladders; whilst in another basin they are high up out of the water, so that their green copper sheathing is almost level with the eye of the passenger; while above his head a long line of bowsprits stretches far over the quay; and from them hang spars and planks as gangway to each ship."

The great revival and expansion of trade which began to gather momentum in the 1840s led to a new phase of docks development. Optimism was reborn. Two Acts of Parliament, passed in 1850 and 1853, gave a new company powers to acquire a large area of pasture and agricultural land in a marshy area between Blackwall Reach and Galleons Reach and to build a new dock there. The company took over 200 acres more than the dock would require so that there would be "pasture accommodation for the large quantities of foreign cattle it was expected would be landed at the docks". It was never so used. But when the Victoria Dock was opened by Prince Albert in 1855 it did have several unique features. It was the first to be built with a direct rail link—to the Great Eastern Railway. It was the first to be equipped with the new telegraph service, so that it always had up-to-date advice of the movements of the new steamships. It was the first to have jetties projecting into the dock instead of straight quay walls; there were eight such jetties, each equipped with hydraulic cranes, so that cargoes could be moved from vessels berthed at one side to lighters waiting at the other. Substantial warehouses were built for the storage of grain and general cargoes.

The Victoria Dock initially attracted shipowners by exempting vessels from dues, except for a nominal rent of one penny per week. Within five years it had attracted more tonnage than any of its rivals. Traffic into enclosed docks in 1860 was:

Victoria	2,682 ships,	850,337 tons
East and West India	1,200 ships,	498,366 tons
London	1,032 ships,	424,338 tons
St Katharine	905 ships,	223,397 tons

London and St Katharine, handicapped by relatively narrow entrances and by lack of railway connections, were left with little other than coastal and near-continental traffic and, as financial difficulties again assailed the docks, these two companies amalgamated in 1864 and took over the new rival Victoria Dock to form the London and St Katharine Docks Company.

Another amalgamation occurred in the same year, on the other side of the river. The Commercial Dock system had been doing well and in 1862 had opened up a new entrance to the river, the Lavender Lock. But the Grand Surrey Docks and Canal Company, despite a reorganisation in 1855 and the opening of a new 16-acres Albion Dock with a new lock and basin in 1860, was in difficulties. In 1864 it was swallowed up by its more prosperous neighbour, to form the Surrey Commercial Dock Company.

Undeterred by these developments, another new company emerged, the Millwall Freehold Land and Dock Company, which proceeded to construct the Millwall Dock, on the Isle of Dogs, immediately south of the West India complex. The theory was that, the Corn Laws having been repealed as part of the movement to free trade and with the new prairie railways just opening up, there would be profit in handling the cargoes of cheap foreign grain. Special facilities were provided for this purpose and a dock with a total water area of 36 acres was constructed, with a 413-feet-long dry dock beside it. The dock was opened on 14th March, 1868 and it attracted a reasonable amount of

The *Thomas King* entering London Dock in 1827 with the first cargo of sugar from the West Indies after the expiration of the exclusive privilege of the West India Dock Company. Oil painting by William John Huggins.   *Courtesy P.L.A.*

A lithograph by William Parrott portraying the West India Dock in 1830, viewed from the south-east.   *Courtesy P.L.A.*

business, but most of it came in the form of Baltic grain accepted at rates so low that they provided no adequate return to the new company, and did much damage to all its rivals.

After this, the story of the enclosed docks in the nineteenth century is a sorry one. It was the great age of Victorian imperialism; during the quarter century from 1875 to 1900 nearly five million square miles of territory and nearly 100 millions of population were added to the Empire, mainly in Africa. Development of the great new territories of Australia and Canada proceeded rapidly. The British operated more than half the total world tonnage of shipping and had more than twice as much tonnage of steamships as the rest of the world together. Trade continued to increase. The atmosphere along the Thames was euphoric. But there were difficulties. The opening of the Suez Canal, in 1869, diverted many Far East cargoes to Mediterranean ports, and from this development the East and West India Dock Company particularly suffered. With the laying of ocean cables and improved communications and with much quicker turn-round of vessels in port because of screw propulsion and the use of steam tugs, it became possible to organise the flow of trade holding much smaller stocks of produce and commodities in London than had earlier been considered necessary.

In assessing these developments and adapting to them, the dock companies showed little skill, for their recipe was to continue as before, but on a bigger

74

and more expensive scale. In 1875 the London and St Katharine Company obtained an Act to build the largest dock in the world, just to the east of the Victoria Dock which it had taken over by amalgamation in 1864. The Royal Albert Dock, as this became known, was opened by the Duke of Connaught, on behalf of Queen Victoria, on 24th June, 1880. It cost £2,200,000 and was a mile and three-quarters long, with a water area of 87 acres, a depth of 27 feet, and 16,500 feet of quays lined by transit sheds served by road and rail facilities. When it was opened the largest ship coming regularly to London was the *Queen*, of 4,457 tons, but the Royal Albert Dock was designed to take vessels of 12,000 tons.

Now competition became so unbridled that the various companies were on a suicide course. Much of the shipping which went into the new Royal Albert Dock came from the South West India Dock upstream, which had been created only in 1866-70 by further improvements to what had originally been the City Canal. The East and West India Dock Company poured in more money to make further improvements there and fought doggedly to keep the South West India Dock busy. Special warehouses were built for more effective display of wool and for a time this dock took most of this business—until in 1887 the London and St Katharine Company improved *their* facilities, whereupon the pampered wool merchants found they could save themselves a

London Dock. This sketch by an anonymous artist conveys the atmosphere of the nineteenth century quays crowded with cargoes in casks and dominated by tall masts and rigging.

Courtesy P.L.A.

six miles journey. Then the South West India Dock provided shed and equipment to attract the timber trade, but this put it into competition with the Surrey Docks, which only a few years before had opened a new Canada Dock of 16 acres, with 46 acres of sheds for timber storage. The Surrey Docks Company was already in stiff competition with the Millwall Dock for grain traffic, having also built four big granaries, with a capacity of 35,000 tons, only eight years after Millwall had made its bid.

The most dramatic, climactic, competitive clash was directly sparked by the opening of the Royal Albert Dock. Not to be outdone by the London and St Katharine's new show-piece, the East and West India Company announced that it would build something better. Before any public announcement was made, secret agents prospected at Tilbury and took options on 450 acres of marshland. A bill was drafted and presented to Parliament and, while it was still being discussed in committee, a provisional contract for construction of new docks at Tilbury was drawn up. There were to be no half-measures. The capital cost was estimated at £2,800,000. There were to be 56 acres of dock water, an entrance through a tidal basin of 19 acres and then a lock measuring 695 by 79½ feet. The depth of water in the basin would never be less than 26 feet and it would be 33 feet in the docks, which meant that any vessel afloat would be able to enter at any state of the tide. The arguments seemed overwhelming; ships would be saved the long pull up the river, with a considerable saving of time and of money on towage and pilotage. The Act went through Parliament in 1882 and within five days the first turf was cut on the site.

A hard bargain was driven with the London, Tilbury and Southend Railway Company; it agreed to build a new depot in the Commercial Road to handle Tilbury cargoes, to lease to the dock company a large warehouse immediately over this depot, and to provide a half-hourly service of passenger trains between London and Tilbury, completing the journey in 35 minutes, as well as all necessary freight trains. On this understanding, the dock company built very little warehouse accommodation at Tilbury, but provided 50 miles of railway track within the dock, laid in front of and behind every transit shed, and with a marshalling yard north of the dock in which to assemble trains. The railway company kept its part of the bargain and built a fine four-floor warehouse of 358,000 square feet in the East End. The Dock Company also reached an understanding with lighterage contractors that they would provide whatever service was required on the river.

Things began to go awry long before the docks were completed. For a start, the rival London and St Katharine Company enlarged the entrance lock to its Royal Albert Dock so that it matched that proposed at Tilbury. There was a great deal of difficulty and dispute during actual construction and at one stage, in 1884, the contractors were ejected from the site and new ones

The Gateway and tower provided for the East India Dock indicates the scale and grandeur which was considered appropriate to the new enterprises.

P.L.A. Collection, Museum of London

brought in, which led to expensive litigation. But the work was completed, the new Tilbury Docks were officially opened on 7th April, 1886 — and within two years its proprietors, the East and West India Docks Company, were in the hands of receivers and managers.

The story is a dismal one of hopes brought to ruins. In the first few months after opening, Tilbury attracted only one regular customer: a line of small German steamers running to Central America once a month. A few other vessels were bribed in by purely nominal charges, but owners of liners using the Royal Albert Dock held back. The master lightermen demanded higher rates and eventually refused to go down river at all, and thus the wharfingers were led to boycott Tilbury traffic. By August 1886 the owners of the fine new docks were desperate. They persuaded the Clan Line to switch from South West India Dock by offering a ten-year contract at half rates. Later, by similar long-term, cut-price arrangements, they secured the Anchor Line to America, the Orient Line to Australia, and three smaller lines. But the rates charged proved ruinous. The rival London and St Katharine Company felt compelled to reduce its charges at the Victoria and Albert Docks to hold what business remained. Consequently, in 1887 the East and West India Company was running at a loss, while the London and St Katharine Company had to cut its dividend to one per cent. Pressure was put on both companies to amalgamate, or at least to reach a working partnership. In March 1888 agreement was reached that the two undertakings should be operated as one, but without an amalgamation of their capital, but this was not secured in time to avoid the appointment of receivers at Tilbury.

From 1888 to the end of 1900 a Joint Committee consisting of ten members drawn from the Board of the London and St Katharine Dock Company and seven drawn from the Board of the East and West India Dock Company administered the undertakings. Profits were divided; of the first £475,000, the London and St Katharine Company took 69 per cent and the East and West India Company 31 per cent, and any additional profits were shared equally. It was a strange interregnum, during which it was sometimes difficult to reconcile the interests of the two parties. Some improvements in dock facilities were, nevertheless, carried through; entrance locks to the West India and South West India docks were widened, warehouses in West India Dock were equipped to provide cold storage, and a new cold store was built adjoining Smithfield Market. One of the major new developments of this period was the shipment of frozen meat and the cargoes brought to London increased from 51,300 tons in 1889 to 171,100 tons in 1900. Eventually, it was appreciated that there was no alternative to complete amalgamation of the companies and so, on 1st January, 1901 a new London and India Docks Company took control. By then the government had set up a Royal Commission to investigate every aspect of the operation of the Port of London.

The decision to refer the problem to a Royal Commission was announced in the House of Commons in May 1900 during the second reading debate of a bill prepared by the dock companies which sought to abolish the "free water clause". It proposed that lighters entering the London and India Docks to discharge or receive goods from vessels docked there should pay fourpence per ton register, and that any goods they carried should be charged at not more than 1s. 6d. per ton. This had always seemed to the dock companies the obvious solution to their difficulties, and they had campaigned against the "free water clause" for half a century and more; but this latest proposal again roused strong opposition from all sides. The "free water clause" was important not only to the lightermen, but to wharfingers as well, and they had become a powerful organisation.

They had first combined formally in 1854, to oppose a project for a new dock at Southwark, but when, in the following year, the London and St Katharine and the India Docks Companies combined to promote a first Parliamentary Bill to destroy the "free water clause", the wharfingers switched their attention to that battle and fought it doggedly thereafter. The

As this poster shows, by 1832 steam packets were providing a regular service along the river and to many other ports.   *Courtesy P.L.A.*

St. Katharine's
STEAM-PACKET-WHARF,
ADJOINING THE TOWER,

Where Passengers embark and land, with Comfort, Personal Security, unexampled Facility, and Despatch, without the Aid, or being exposed to the Risk, of Boat-Conveyance, and also without any Charge whatsoever.

ELEGANTLY-FITTED AND COMMODIOUS STEAM-PACKETS,

Of acknowledged SPEED, proceed to and from the following Places, at stated Hours, with the most undeviating Punctuality :—

Gravesend, Northfleet, Southend, Sheerness, Chatham, Herne-Bay, Margate, Ramsgate, Walton, Harwich, Ipswich, Scarborough, Whitby, Redcar, Durham, Darlington, Stockton-upon-Tees, Leith, Edinburgh, Dundee, &c. &c.

The Public generally, and Persons of Rank and Distinction in particular, continue to give a decided Preference to this Establishment, not only on account of the very SUPERIOR AND PECULIAR ACCOMMODATION provided, as compared with that of any other Place at the Water-Side in the Port of London, but from the circumstance also of the St. Katharine's Wharf being the first to afford such inestimable Accommodation.

The Approaches, both by Land and Water, possess unexampled Convenience.

Passengers landing at this Wharf are exempt from the exorbitant Rates of Porterage, to which Landing Places between the Tower and London Bridge are subject.

A Hackney Coach-Stand adjoining the Entrance-Gate.

For further Particulars apply to Mr. MORETON, Superintendent, at the Wharf.

1832.

competition between the dock companies and the wharfingers was as cut-throat as it was between the dock companies themselves, for large firms had now taken control of the riverside wharves and warehouses, and had equipped them with facilities matching those in the docks. By 1898 it was estimated that less than 20 per cent of all goods discharged in the docks were paying charges to the dock companies; the rest was going overside into barges for transfer to river wharves or for immediate delivery to consignees.

The headlong rush during the nineteenth century to open up impressive new docks was related not only to the steady expansion of trade, which, indeed, was insufficient to sustain the new facilities. It was stimulated by a transformation in the nature of shipping using the port. During this century sail was almost completely supplanted by steam. In 1800 the largest vessels sailing into the Thames were the East Indiamen of 1,200 tons, and speed of turn-round was not an important factor. A round voyage for one of these vessels from London to Calcutta never took less than eighteen months, so that there seemed nothing disproportionate in a discharging period of six to eight weeks. The largest East Indiaman, fully loaded, drew 23 feet and there was insufficient channel depth for it above Erith, which is fifteen miles downstream from London Bridge. Sufficient cargo was discharged, therefore, in Long Reach, below Erith, to reduce the draught to 17 feet, and the vessel then proceeded to Blackwall, where the balance of cargo was transferred into lighters. By 1900 steam was triumphant, though it had not yet banished sail; some liners of 12,000 to 15,000 tons were coming to the Thames and so much money was invested in them that quick turn-round had become an important factor.

Despite the challenge of steam, the sailing vessels had their heyday in the nineteenth century, throughout which the Thames maintained its proud tradition of ship-building. At Blackwall, in particular, under a succession of Johnsons, Perrys and Greens, and throughout almost three centuries, fleets of magnificent wooden ships took the water. In George III's time the Blackwall yard was described as "the most capacious in the kingdom and probably in the world". With the increasing use of iron, however, shipbuilding moved to the north and most of the Thames yards closed; the Blackwall tradition, however, is preserved to this day in ship repair yards on the original site, though ship construction ceased there in 1907.

The change from sail to steam gathered momentum in the decade 1850-60. The first steam collier appeared in 1851, within three years there were 36 of them, and by 1865 practically all the coal traffic to London was handled by steam — well over four million tons a year. Each of the new steam colliers carried 580 to 600 tons, which was twice the capacity of each of the sailing vessels they replaced. The balance swung decisively from sail to steam between 1865 and 1875, during which decade the total tonnage of steam

The Pool of London. Lively activity in the Pool in 1862 is shown in this lithograph.

Courtesy P.L.A.

coming into the port increased from 2,900,000 to 5,100,000, while the tonnage under sail declined from 3,800,000 to 3,600,000. Although ship-building moved away, London as a port was a pace-setter in this change and about half the steam vessels in Britain were registered there. At the same time, it regularly received some of the finest sailing vessels of all time, fleets of clippers like the *Cutty Sark* (which can now be seen at Greenwich) and, by the turn of the century, great four-masted, barque-rigged ships 400 feet long which could carry 5,000 tons of cargo.

Steam enabled the authorities to improve efficiency of operation on the river — even the sailing vessels could now move in the stream at all times with the aid of steam tugs — but maintenance of a navigational channel of sufficient depth proved a problem and caused much controversy. It was the responsibility of the Thames Conservators, who had been appointed in 1857 to replace the City Corporation's Navigation Committee. During the early years after their appointment the Conservators worked hard to remove shoals, to provide better moorings, to regulate the traffic on the river, and to improve piers and landing places. But still an average tide provided no more than twenty feet of water in the channel up to London Bridge, and then only for about three hours. At low tide there were limiting depths of less than twelve feet in Barking and Woolwich Reaches. Once the Royal Albert Dock had been opened in 1880 the demands for deepening of the channel became more insistent. The investment in the new dock made no sense unless there was a 30 feet channel to its entrance in Galleons Reach, whereas in fact, the available depth was only 18 feet. The big new ships in the American trade frequently had a loaded draught of 30 feet, the dock had sufficient depth to contain them, but the river could not carry them there. At about this same time there was discussion of deepening the Suez Canal from 26 to 30 feet, which added strength to the dock companies' and ship-owners' case.

In 1887 thirty-six impatient shipping and marine insurance companies made a joint appeal to the Conservancy Board to improve the channel all the way from Gravesend to London; eventually, but not until 1894, the Board of Trade appointed a Lower Thames Navigation Commission to investigate. In March 1896 this Commission recommended provision of a 30-feet channel "at least" to Gravesend, and the Conservators went to work. By 1900, when the problems was overtaken by the appointment of the Royal Commission to investigate the port in general, they had managed to deepen only to 26 feet to Gravesend, to 22 feet to the Albert Dock entrance, and to 18 feet to Millwall.

It is fair to record that the Conservators had many other urgent matters to occupy their attention during the second half of the nineteenth century, some of them arguably even more important than the improvement of the navigation channel. London had expanded at a spectacular pace and the population was now pouring more filth into the Thames than was caused by trade or industry. In the early years of the century the river had been clear and sweet; as late as 1807 Lord Byron claimed that he had swum in it for three miles from Lambeth to London Bridge. In 1847 cesspools were made illegal in the capital, with the result that the whole of its sewage thereafter flowed into the river. The Conservators, upon their appointment, had to attend to the control of countless big new sewers and drains.

If the opportunities and the achievements of the nineteenth century were on a scale which had previously been undreamt of, so were the difficulties and the disappointments. In 1900 London was undeniably the greatest port in the world in terms of its trade; nowhere else were there such magnificent docks, so large or so well-equipped; nowhere else could one see so impressive a procession of shipping, nor so much of it home-built and locally registered. Yet almost all the commercial enterprises which had built and operated this port were in utter disarray, apparently incapable of solving the problems which clouded its future.

London Dock in the 1880s. This photograph captures the full flavour of Victorian dockland.
Radio Times Hulton Picture Library

Viscount Devonport of Whittington, P.C., the first Chairman of the Port of London Authority (from 1909 to 1925). Portrait by Z. Nemethy, after Philip de Laszlo. *Courtesy P.L.A.*

CHAPTER FIVE

Reorganisation and Set-back

THE task of designing a new order in the Port of London occupied the Royal Commission appointed in 1900 for two full years. Though its recommendations were clear and logical, their implementation was delayed for almost seven more years, so that throughout most of the opening decade of the present century the port lacked firm and purposeful management. Notable improvements in port facilities were made, nonetheless. Serious reorganisation was put in hand only in 1909 and was soon afterwards interrupted by the First World War. When that was over, the momentum of reconstruction and expansion had scarcely been re-established when the world economic crisis of 1929-31 destroyed something like half the trade of the port. Then before recovery was complete, Britain was involved in the Second World War, from which she emerged victorious but bankrupt. Thus were the vicissitudes of the nineteenth century re-enacted in the twentieth, but with a pace and drama so much greater than in the earlier period that they were like a technicolour movie beside a sepia print. In such circumstances, the achievements of those who managed the port in the first half of this century were very remarkable.

The task of the Royal Commission of 1900 was defined in its terms of reference thus: "to inquire into the present administration of the port and the water approaches thereto, the adequacy of the accommodation provided for vessels and the loading and unloading thereof, the system of charges for such accommodation and the arrangements for warehousing dutiable goods, and to report whether any change or improvement in regard to any of the above matters is necessary for the promotion of the trade of the port and the public interest". The Commission sat on 31 days and heard 114 witnesses, but only four organisations submitted detailed proposals for the future management of the port: the City Corporation, the London and India Dock Company, the London Chamber of Commerce, and the London County Council (which had been brought into existence twelve years earlier).

A common theme which ran through much of the evidence was that London was losing trade to other ports where, it was claimed, greater efficiency had been achieved. The spectacular development of industry close to the northern coalfields had, of course, had much to do with the expansion of the ports of Liverpool, Glasgow and Hull; the value of traffic through Liverpool now almost equalled that through London. An ominous new development was that Hamburg, Antwerp and Rotterdam were increasing their business, in percentage terms, much faster than London. The Chamber of Commerce declared that these ports, which were owned by state or municipality, had lower warehousing charges and faster handling times.

An apologist for the performance of London at the time, Sir Joseph Broodbank, commented:

"That London was a slow port in obtaining deliveries of cargoes had to be admitted, but this was due chiefly to the employment of barges taking deliveries. Barges provide the cheapest method or conveyance in the port, carrying goods for thirty miles at the same cost as would be payable for one mile of road conveyance. But the method of conveyance is undoubtedly slow. In London, with its scattered areas and long distances, it is, however, the only practical form of conveyance for 95 per cent of the goods discharged from ships in the port . . . The delays complained of arise largely from the necessities of the situation and, amongst others, from the fact that London cargoes are generally mixed cargoes, and in order that they may be sorted for delivery such cargoes are first landed, instead of being delivered over the ship's side direct to craft . . . As barges are employed, it is necessary to have parcels completely sorted in order to get full freights, and this cannot be done until after the ship is emptied. Hence, deliveries cannot commence till five or six days after the ship's arrival in dock."

London was unique among ports in its dependence upon lighters; nearly eighty per cent by tonnage of imports were delivered into them. The remainder were landed on quays in the docks or at riverside wharves, and then delivered by rail or road, possibly after being stored for a while. The lighters were ubiquitous. They were in the docks, loading cargoes overside direct from incoming vessels or from the quays on to which they had been temporarily landed to assist sorting and grouping; they were at all the riverside wharves taking direct deliveries overside, and they were alongside all vessels mooring in the river to discharge. The lighters carried their cargoes from dock to warehouse, from ship to wharf, from quay to quay, from ship to ship, from river to canal: their movements were myriad and complex.

All witnesses appearing before the Royal Commission agreed that efficiency could not be improved unless there was a co-ordinated control of the port. In its report, published on 16th June, 1902, the Commission recommended the creation of a single public authority which should be representative of all port users. Within a few months the government prepared a bill with proposals to establish a Port of London Authority, and this received a second reading in 1903 and was committed to a Joint Committee of Lords and Commons. Then followed years of procrastination. Crowded out of one session, the bill was transferred to the following one, and then quietly

The Docks from the air. 1. London and St Katharine, photographed in 1960.

dropped. The delay had permitted various vested interests to mobilise opposition, so that the measure had become highly controversial. The Unionist government of the day was in difficulties with tariff reform and was staggering to defeat in 1905. In the vacuum thus created, the dock companies reintroduced their own bill to charge duties on lighters entering the docks, while the London County Council promoted a bill to municipalise the port. Everything seemed to be back in the melting pot, even to the extent of renewed debate about the rival merits of enclosed docks and riverside wharves. When a new Liberal government was formed in December 1905 the President of the Board of Trade, Mr David Lloyd George, initiated discussions with the dock companies about the compensation they should receive; it was agreed that they would accept Port Stock and that this would not be secured upon the London rates. Other problems were gradually solved by negotiation and Lloyd George introduced a new Port of London Bill in the Commons on 2nd April, 1908. Eleven days later Asquith formed a new Ministry and Mr Winston Churchill took over from Lloyd George at the Board of Trade and piloted the bill through its second reading without a division. The Parliamentary Secretary, Sir Hudson Ewbanke Kearley, then took charge of the measure, and steered it through a Joint Committee of Lords and Commons, and it received the Royal Assent on 21st December, 1908.

Twenty-eight members were appointed to the Board of the new Authority. Ten were nominated to represent public bodies: four from the London County Council, two from the City Corporation, two from the Board of Trade, one each from the Admiralty and Trinity House. The eighteen others were elected by the private users of the port: shipowners, merchants, wharfingers and owners of river craft. The Chairman and Vice-Chairman could be elected by the members, if they wished, from outside their number. The much-disputed "free water clause" continued to operate, but the P.L.A. was authorised to impose a registration fee on lighters and other small craft (licensing of which was transferred to the Authority from the Watermen's Company). The P.L.A. was also given a right to acquire by compulsory purchase any private wharf or warehouse along the river. Trinity House was left with the responsibility for river pilotage, which it had enjoyed by charter since 1514, and for buoying and lighting. The Metropolitan Police was responsible for patrol of the tideway. The City Corporation remained the Health Authority, with responsibility for appropriate supervision of cargoes and passengers.

On 1st March, 1909 the P.L.A. took over from the dock companies five separate dock complexes: London and St Katharine, Surrey Commercial, India and Millwall, the Royals and Tilbury. Between them, they had an area of nearly 3,000 acres, including 700 acres of enclosed water, about thirty miles of quays, and four dry docks. It also took over the property, powers and duties of the Thames Conservancy Board. Thus it acquired statutory powers to levy

The Docks from the air. 2. The Surrey Commercial group, photographed in the early 1960s.

Courtesy P.L.A.

tonnage dues on all ships entering the port, charges on all goods passing through it and storage and service charges for the use of warehouses. The dock companies received £22,362,976 and the P.L.A. was empowered to raise capital from the public of £27 millions. In operating the port, the P.L.A. was to use any excess of revenue over expenses, after payment of interest, to carry through port improvements or to reduce port dues and charges.

When the Board of the P.L.A. met for the first time, it had to take note of developments in the port in the years since the Royal Commission had reported. The wharfingers had gained ground; the river was lined almost continuously with over three hundred private wharves, with fifteen miles of quays and with a capital value which certainly exceeded £10 millions. Hay's Wharf, for example, was the largest single area in the port handling general provisions, including butter, bacon and tea and its warehouses could hold as much as those of St Katharine Dock. Other principal wharves were Fresh Wharf, discharging vessels bringing fruit for the nearby market in Pudding Lane; the General Steam Navigation Company's wharves at St Katharine and Irongate; Morocco Wharf at Wapping, with berths for the Royal Mail Company's vessels trading with Morocco; Mark Brown's and Davis Wharves, just above Tower Bridge on the south bank; and Bellamy's Wharf, opposite the Shadwell entrance to London Dock, which handled large quantities of grain. The P.L.A. did not acquire any of these wharves, but it certainly could not be indifferent to their activities.

The old dock companies, although naturally disinclined to make major decisions during the years of uncertainty, had carried through some important improvements. A silo granary had been erected on the south side of the Royal Victoria Dock, where the firms of Joseph Rank Ltd. and William Vernon and Sons built themselves large flour mills. At about the same time a 13-floor Central Granary soaring above Millwall Dock introduced exciting new technology to the port: pneumatic discharge of grain cargoes from ships' holds direct to any part of the seven and a quarter acres of storage floors. Until 1903 all grain had been unloaded by bucket or skip, used with cranes; now eight "elephant trunk" tubes sucked 300 tons an hour ashore.

The other major development had been the opening of a new, enlarged Greenland Dock south of the river, 2,250 feet long and 450 feet across, with a water area of 22 acres. It had been planned before the turn of the century, but was not completed until 1904. At the official opening the tug *Canada*, with the dock directors aboard, entered ceremonially ahead of the first timber ship, but unfortunately insufficient other timber ships followed behind. In 1906 a new policy was adopted. Taking advantage of the dock's position only two miles from the centre of the provision trade in Tooley Street, the company built cold storage facilities and persuaded two Canadian lines to bring in cargoes which had previously gone to the Victoria Dock. In retaliation, the London and

Courtesy P.L.A.

The Docks from the air. 3. West India and Millwall, photographed in 1962.

India Company offered to take softwood at 25 per cent below Surrey rates. Thus, as private enterprise rounded off an impressive record of construction in the port, it simultaneously demonstrated again its self-destructive capacity. It probably was no satisfaction to anyone that an interesting essay in public enterprise at this time was equally unsuccessful. The London County Council, which had shown some keenness to run the port as a whole, tried its hand at a service of river steamers. It bought thirty of them for £200,000, operated them at a loss between 1905 and 1909 and, with a change of control of the Council, sold off the fleet for only £18,000.

It is safe to assume that nothing of the history of failure in any way deterred the first Chairman of the Port of London Authority. Sir Hudson Kearley, who became Viscount Devonport in 1917, was a self-made business-man of fifty-three who had acquired wealth and entered politics at a comparatively early age, and who had achieved junior ministerial office. His duties as Parliamentary Secretary at the Board of Trade during the passage of the Act creating the P.L.A. had provided him with an extremely detailed knowledge of the port and of those concerned with it. He was a man of forceful character and inflexible resolve, to a degree which at a later stage embarrassed some of his associates. In the early, formative years, however, no-one could have been a more powerful instrument of progress and reform. When he called his colleagues together for the first time, in the boardroom of the old London and India Docks Company in Leadenhall Street, he already had a clear programme in mind. There were years of neglect to be made up. The new Chief Engineer reported that it would cost £735,000 to put dock properties and premises into good order, and this patching-up was commenced immediately. A sum of £426,000 was voted for the purchase of dredging equipment and work began on the improvement of the navigational channel to provide 20 feet of water to the Royal Albert Dock and 14 feet to London Bridge. A new pumping station to raise the level of water in the Royal Docks by thirty inches was constructed at Galleons Entrance, the north quay of London Western Dock was widened and a new double-storey shed built, and the Millwall Dry Dock was extended—all during 1911-12.

By January 1911 a programme estimated to cost £14,426,000 had been prepared, and arranged in three parts, the first phase, which was costed at £3,896,700, being vigorously pushed forward within a year. The boldest decision was to construct an entirely new dock, south of the Royal Albert Dock, on a scale which would enable it to receive liners of up to 30,000 tons. Improvements were commenced in every dock in the system: reconstruction of the north quay and sheds at West India Import and Export Docks, rebuilding of one entrance to London Dock and construction of a new ferro-concrete jetty there, extension of the main dock at Tilbury, and improvement of pumping installations to heighten water levels in several docks.

The Docks from the air. 4. East India Docks, photographed in 1947.   *Aerofilms Limited*

The Board had also to face other problems than those of dock construction and improvement. The various police forces which had been taken over from the dock companies needed to be integrated and reorganised. Clerical staff had to be redeployed and augmented to deal with the new activities, but accommodation was lacking. They were scattered in old buildings, many of which had been warehouses, and the ambience was Dickensian. "The Deposit Office in Crutched Friars was in an old derelict warehouse to which the only access was a narrow iron spiral staircase," recalls one of the staff at that time. "The warehouse ceiling was no more than seven feet high, and the windows were old-fashioned with small panes and grilles outside. There were high desks and stools, with gas lights on top of the desks, as the ceiling was too low for them to be hung. We were so cramped that if anyone wished to go to the toilet, everyone had to get off his stool to let him pass." It was easy enough to bring in telephones and typewriters, but there was going to have to be a new headquarters building. A contest was announced, 170 architects submitted designs, in 1912 a scheme was approved, and work had commenced on the Tower Hill site by the following year. In all these matters, Kearley was indefatigable; he kept six committees of the Board constantly occupied and meeting weekly; a new recruit to the P.L.A staff in those early years noted that "management wrought with fiendish efficiency, the Board members twisted the tails of management to perform the impossible".

The Board also had to concern itself, of course, with revenue. It produced a new tariff of charges and now, with its authority to licence lighters and small craft, it fixed charges of sixpence per registered ton for dumb craft (un-powered barges), eightpence for sailing craft, sixpence per ton plus £2 for each steam barge, and £5 for each tug, and between them these smaller vessels contributed £320,000 a year to revenue.

By the time war broke out in 1914 a very large part of the first phase of reconstruction had been completed. Nine dredgers had been constantly at work and immense quantities of material had been taken in 21 steam hoppers to be dumped at sea. Forty-six sunken vessels had been cleared from the river-bed within a period of one year. The new sheds and improved quays in West India and East India Docks and the work in the London Dock were all completed. One new berth had been finished at Tilbury and it could take the largest vessels afloat, and it was estimated that about eighteen months' work remained to complete the magnificent new dock just south of the Royal Albert Dock. This was progress at an impressive pace, and the P.L.A.'s financial results looked promising too, as these figures show:

	1909-10	1913-14
Tonnage of ships entered and cleared (foreign and coastwise)	35,151,799	40,080,282
Tonnage using docks	17,436,097	18,517,590
Revenue	£2,631,676	£3,434,453
Working expenses	£1,766,926	£2,217,882
	£ 864,750	£1,216,571
Surplus after paying interest on Port Stock	£ 57,929	£ 283,845

Although the shadow of war had been evident for some time, Britain was enjoying prosperity. Dividend income from capital investment overseas reached £188 millions and invisible earnings from shipping were also at a peak. The total value of U.K. imports and exports, excluding coastwise traffic, was £1,343 millions in 1912 and well over a quarter of this (£383 millions) came through London. Up to half a million tons of goods at a time were stored in P.L.A. warehouses and the Authority's staff sorted, sampled, graded and prepared for market a large proportion of these goods. No other port authority in the world fulfilled such a range of services on such a scale. The entrepôt functions of London were at a peak. Wool was the most important single commodity, with £25 millions-worth handled annually. The great London wool sales took place at the Wool Exchange in Coleman Street or at the Commercial Sale Rooms in Mincing Lane, but the wool remained in the dock warehouses. Either the buyers went there in advance to inspect it, or they

The Docks from the air. 5. The Royal group, photographed in 1962.

Courtesy P.L.A.

depended upon samples taken to them. It was much the same with a whole range of goods: grain, sugar, tea, wines and spirits, tobacco. The buyers came from all over the world; taking wool as an example, two-fifths of the sales went to foreign buyers and the balance to British manufacturers.

It is doubtful if at any other period of its history the Port of London has displayed such a range of fascinating activity and of specialist skills as in those days immediately before the First World War. A detailed survey is provided by an official "Guide for the use of visitors" published in 1913. The biggest cargo flows were handled in the Royal Albert and Victoria Docks, through which passed nearly half the tonnage using the docks; but the most exotic cargoes were concentrated in the London and St Katharine Docks, which constituted a museum of the products of every corner of the world.

Starting our survey at the mouth of the river, Tilbury was in the grip of extension work in 1913. It was busy at this time, with 67 hydraulic travelling cranes shifting the products of Asia and Australia through its 24 transit sheds and on to rail wagons. Liners of 12,000 to 15,000 tons sailed regularly to India, China, Burma and Australia and there was a daily boat to Ostend and a service to Hamburg. To cater for these passengers and their relatives there was a 100-bed hotel, with pleasant gardens and tennis courts and splendid views of the river. Quite separately, Tilbury Dock boasted a restaurant with first, second and third-class refreshment rooms.

Further up-river, the Victoria and Albert Docks had become a forest of cranes — 180 of them altogether, including two that floated in the docks. The three and a quarter million square feet of warehouses and sheds were always full of grain, frozen meat and tobacco. At any one time there were 15,000 to 20,000 tons of tobacco in bond there. The frozen meat stores were the world's largest; from them the carcases were moved into insulated rail wagons which came alongside. The railway had become a major feature of the docks complex: there were extensive sidings for marshalling and there were actually four passenger stations on P.L.A. property. Trains from Fenchurch Street called at Tidal Basin, at the west end of the Victoria Dock; Custom House, station for the Victoria Dock offices; Connaught Road, at the west end of the Albert Dock; Central Station, for Albert Dock general offices; Manor Way, east end of the Albert Dock; and Galleons, for the basin. Near the basin there was "a small first-class hotel" and the railway also provided a buffet.

The East India Dock in 1913 was virtually out of commission because of the scale of reconstruction in hand there. But up-stream at the West India Import Dock the north quay, in front of the great Georgian warehouses, had been widened and provided with travelling cranes and the activity was intense. The first three warehouses, and the quays which fronted them, received boards and planks which would be used for furniture; the fourth, sixth and seventh warehouses handled sugar; the fifth one was a depot for frozen meat

The Docks from the air. 6. Tilbury Docks, photographed in 1951. The riverside area at the left of the picture later saw the development of the Bulk Grain Terminal, the Northfleet Hope Container Terminal and a new dock with berths for unitised cargoes.   *Aerofilms Limited*

from Australia, New Zealand and Argentina; the eighth and ninth were equipped with bucket elevators to handle grain and seed in bulk; and the tenth warehouse was an Admiralty stores depot. The Rum Quay occupied the greater part of the south quay of the Import Dock, with a sickly, sweet odour rising from the vaults below; these were 1,040 feet long and 154 feet wide and provided storage for 40,000 puncheons, of 100 to 120 gallons each: the vats used for blending could hold 58,000 gallons at a time. Coopers walked the vaults every day, sounding the casks with their hammers. In another part of the Import Dock electric travellers and cranes swung enormous logs of mahogany, up to 60 feet in length and ten tons in weight, which came from Africa, the West Indies and South and Central America, and also teak from India, Siam and Burma.

The two other docks in the West India complex had a special interest at this time, but, as they offered none of the new wonders of that age, they were not drawn to the special attention of visitors. The South Dock was the stronghold of sail in the port, and most of the large sailing vessels remaining in the East India and Colonial trade loaded at its north quay or discharged on the south side. Vessels which had been laid up filled much of the space in the West India Export Dock while the work of widening and improving its north quay prevented more active use.

Millwall Dock, nearby, handled two-fifths of the grain arriving in London, most of it from the Baltic and the Black Sea, and sent it on its way in 400 railway wagons despatched every week. There were 48 miles of railway track on the dock premises.

In the Surrey Commercial Docks timber imported from the Baltic, the White Sea, the United States and Canada made it "the largest emporium for wood goods in the world", in the words of the 1913 Guide. This timber could be stored under cover in 50 acres of sheds, or piled on the 200 acres of open ground, or floated in the 70 acres of ponds. Grain came from the Baltic, the Black Sea, North America and the River Plate and was transferred by bucket elevators into seven huge, gaunt, brick granaries standing four-square beside the murky water, or, alternatively, into lighters. With the introduction of vessels with refrigerated holds, the Surrey Commercial had provided new facilities to handle Canadian bacon, which arrived in cases of twelve sides weighing about six hundredweights. Cheese and general produce also went into the two million cubic feet of storage, where temperatures were controlled at between 15° and 55°F.

Finally, there were the London and St Katharine Docks, the nearest to the City, and the Cutler Street and Commercial Road warehouses which were closely associated with them. London and St Katharine together handled £8 millions worth of wool, each year — about 40 per cent of all such imports through the port. This meant 500,000 to 600,000 bales, each weighing almost

The red-sailed Thames barges were a special feature of the river scene for centuries. There were enough of them left to play an important part in the evacuation of British troops from Dunkirk in 1940. A few have been preserved, and examples may be seen in the St Katharine yacht basin.

P.L.A. Collection, Museum of London

three hundredweight and containing the shearings of sixty sheep. The dock warehouses had 32 acres of floor space for sorting and storage and before each of the five wool sales each year the bales were opened, graded and lotted. The actual sales took place at the London Wool Exchange in Coleman Street. During the period of the sales, about 1,200 labourers were employed on this work alone.

Tea was dealt with at St Katharine, Cutler Street and Commercial Road. Every year about 32,000 tons of it arrived from India, Ceylon and China in a total of 700,000 packages: chests containing 1 cwt 14 lbs, half-chests containing 2 quarters 14 lbs, boxes containing 1 quarter or, in the case of China tea, wrapped in matting. With the latter, information about the contents was brushed on to the matting with ink, and the chests had these details cut into the wood with a scribing iron. In the presence of Customs officers, P.L.A. staff removed the lids of the chests or bored the matted packages and inspected the contents. These were then weighed, sampled and sorted. Often the tea was "bulked"—turned out on to the floor and thoroughly mixed with wooden spades to even out the quality; at such times the floors were covered with immense heaps of tea. Finally, it was laid down in rows for the inspection of the brokers who would sell it, after which chests and packages were closed up, numbered and stocked away until delivery should be requested.

London Dock handled the wine and brandy trade of the port. On arrival the casks were deposited from the ships on a large area near the wool warehouse, known as "The Crescent", where it was gauged by the Customs. It was then removed to the sixteen acres of wine vaults below the quays. There was room there for 105,000 pipes of wine (a pipe was usually 105 gallons) stored at 55° to 60°F along 28¼ miles of gangways. There were 28 vats for blending, holding 63,000 gallons between them, and a great deal of port, sherry and Madeira was handled. The brandy vaults occupied a further four acres. There was a Bottling Department which drew enough wines and spirits from the casks to fill 63,000 dozen bottles in the year 1912.

Rubber was another important cargo in the London Dock, and rapid growth of this business took place in the pre-1914 period. Rubber and gutta-percha cargoes were turned out on to the north quay of the West Dock from the ships, and there they were weighed and sorted. Samples of about two pounds weight were placed in canvas bags and taken to the Mincing Lane brokers, and the remainder was placed on display in three special show sheds, with specially-designed overhead lighting. It remained there for three or four days, at the most, before being removed to three acres of cool vaults; skilled staff could deal in this way with a cargo worth £60,000 to £70,000 in the course of a few days.

From the appearance of the first paddle steamers, Londoners took to the river and until 1966 there was a daily service from the City to the estuary. The *Royal Daffodil*, seen here early in the present century, was a favourite vessel.   *P.L.A. Collection, Museum of London*

Now we may look, with the aid of the 1913 Guide, at some of the more exotic cargoes of that time. The spices which had so excited the Elizabethans and enriched the East India merchants still arrived in fascinating variety: cloves from the Moluccas, Java, Sumatra, Zanzibar and Mauritius; nutmeg from Singapore, Penang, Madagascar and the West Indies; cinnamon bark, tied in bundles, from Ceylon, and cinchona bark, to produce quinine, from Peru; iodine, also from South America; quicksilver, in iron bottles, from Spain and California, to be used in scientific instruments and for silvering mirrors; and the full range of gums and oils — gum arabic for adhesives, gum cowrie and gum copal for making varnish, gum benjamin for use in perfumery and soap, gum kino used in colouring, and gum alibanum burned as incense. All of these found their way into the huge warehouses at London Dock, where they were handled by men whose specialised knowledge was unmatched anywhere else in the world.

There was also the Ivory House, into which 250 to 300 tons of ivory, valued at £300,000 to £400,000, was shipped each year. Most of it came from Africa, often in tusks nine feet long which weighed well over a hundredweight, but there was also "fossil ivory" from long-extinct mammoths which were being unearthed from the frozen soil of Siberia. The ivory was weighed, examined, classified and laid out for the inspection of the buyers who in due time would arrange for it to be transformed into piano keys and billiard balls and decorations of various kinds. Ivory sales took place four times a year.

St Katharine Dock still had an indigo house, though by 1913 that trade was in decline as the chemical companies developed aniline dyes. In the East Indies and in South America the juice was boiled out of the plant, and the deep blue powder which was thus obtained was compressed into small rectangular blocks measuring about three inches by two inches. These were shipped to London in three-hundredweight chests. Many believed that indigo was still the best base for dyes for woollen cloth.

Not far from the indigo warehouse was the scent factory, where extracts of flowers, mixed with fat, were imported from San Remo and other places. Special machinery installed at the dock separated the essences from the fat and then mixed them with alcohol; this process of manufacture was carried out here in bonded premises, so that some of the scent could be exported without payment of duty on the alcohol used. South of the scent factory there was a large quay which was always covered with blocks and slabs of fine marble imported from Italy.

The most remarkable trades, however, were in shells and feathers. An entire warehouse floor in St Katharine was devoted to shells imported from every region of the world. They were sorted, weighed, valued and lotted for sale, and then placed on display. Mother-of-pearl required good overhead lighting for inspection, while tortoiseshell needed side lighting. Display rooms

In August 1939 the 34,000 tons *Mauretania* berthed in King George V Dock after completing her maiden round crossing of the Atlantic. A hundred thousand people watched the liner enter the port.

Popperfoto

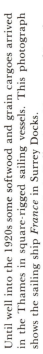

Until well into the 1920s some softwood and grain cargoes arrived in the Thames in square-rigged sailing vessels. This photograph shows the sailing ship *France* in Surrey Docks.

P.L.A. Collection, Museum of London

were specially designed to provide the ideal conditions and every other month buyers flocked into them and purchased four or five thousand tons of shells at each of the regular sales. Tortoise-shell from the West Indies often fetched £10 a pound, though the average price was about 35 shillings a pound, and mother-of-pearl sold for anything between £4 and £14 a hundredweight. The shells were used for inlaid and ornamental furniture, for card cases, purses, and toilet and ornamental articles of many kinds.

The sorting, storage and marketing of feathers was at the Cutler Street warehouse, and over £3 millions a year changed hands in this trade. Not only feathers but also the skins of birds arrived from many countries. South Africa sent large quantities of ostrich feathers; it is difficult to imagine conversation more esoteric than that between the P.L.A. staff and the dealers. "Boos" were the black and white feathers from a male bird, "feminas" the mixed-colour plumage from the hen. The best feathers were the 34 taken from the wing of the ostrich, which were cut every eight months. Each of the six feather sales every year ended with what were called "fancies", which included plumes from the bird of paradise and from the osprey, the best of which realised £14 per ounce. Bird skins were used by milliners, but also by naturalists and for making flies for fishermen, and millions of them arrived each year, including parrots, Himalayan pheasant, humming birds and jays.

This fascinating variety of activity in the port was carried forward by an equally interesting variety of men. Most were veterans from the old dock companies, adapting to new circumstances. Senior managers, down to the rank of principal warehouse-keepers, came to work wearing silk hats and frock coats. Clerks, most of whom were known as "writers"—there were first, second and third-class writers—wore three-piece suits and either bowlers or, in summer, straw hats. Many dock labourers wore bowlers, too, though caps were more popular. Trams and buses brought the experts in world trade in wine, wool, feathers and shells from neat little semi-detached homes in Ilford and Chingford and Woodford. Relations between dock labourers and "the staff" were relaxed and friendly, notwithstanding the fact that the labourers waited each day at the morning calls at the dock gates for perhaps only a couple of hours work at sevenpence an hour, while the clerks earned a regular one pound a week for a regular forty-eight hours work. The docks were a hive of industry, with ships occupying every berth almost continuously, the quays crowded with people, the warehouses attended constantly by horse-vans or railway wagons.

The First World War undermined some of the more colourful trades of the port, and changes in taste and fashion and the progress of chemistry drove many of them into oblivion. The war which speeded some part of this transformation slowed down much of the work of changing the physical aspect of the port as a whole. Work on the giant new basin south of the Royal Albert

Horse vans survived until the Second World War. Here they are seen waiting inside the main entrance to London Dock.　　　　　　　　　　*P.L.A. Collection, Museum of London*

Dock came to a standstill, to be resumed only in the summer of 1918, when the Admiralty urgently needed additional facilities for the repair of torpedoed ships. River dredging ceased altogether from the outbreak of hostilities, because the dredgers were required elsewhere. Construction of a new river jetty at Tilbury went forward intermittently until the summer of 1918, but was then interrupted for a long interval. In 1917 a terrible explosion at a munitions factory in Silvertown caused heavy damage at the Victoria Dock and £250,000 was spent on reconstruction during the following two years. Apart from this, war-time damage in the port was minimal; the official estimate was £3,239. Though there were "incidents", the river was not much disturbed; indeed, during the summers of 1915 to 1918 inclusive the P.L.A. thought it appropriate to provide two steamers for river trips for wounded soldiers! The ordinary traffic of the port was not seriously affected until 1917, when the enemy submarine campaign diverted a good deal of shipping to west coast ports.

The war over, Lord Devonport, as the Chairman had become, returned with vigour to the interrupted task of reconstruction. The first project carried to a triumphal completion was the new dock, which was officially opened by King George V on 8th July, 1921, and named after him. It was so enormous that it added ten per cent to the area of enclosed dock water in the port. The entrance lock at Galleons Reach was 800 feet long by 100 feet wide by 45 feet deep and was constructed so that it could be divided into two separate locks of 580 feet and 250 feet or, alternatively, extended by the use of a floating caisson to 910 feet. Through this impressive entrance liners moved into a basin which was three-quarters of a mile long and which tapered in width from 710 feet at

104

the eastern end to 500 feet at the western end. The south side of this area was laid out in an entirely novel way, with seven "dolphins", or jetties, of reinforced concrete, each 520 feet long and 32 feet wide, built 32 feet out from, and parallel to, the quayside. Vessels berthed on the outside of these dolphins to discharge into lighters using the 32-feet channel. On the north side of the dock there were six substantial two-storey sheds or warehouses designed for quick transfer of cargoes to either rail or road haulage. The King George V Dock completed the complex familiarly known thereafter as "the Royals", which for many years was without equal anywhere in the world. The combined water area was 245 acres and all three docks were interconnected.

The next post-war milestone for the P.L.A. was the official opening, fifteen months later, of its new headquarters building on Tower Hill. The work had been entrusted to Sir Edwin Cooper, F.R.I.B.A., and the result was a building which featured a great columned portico, a main tower 174 feet high, with groups of heroic statuary, including Father Thames, and a rotunda 110 feet in diameter and 67 feet high. Staff who had grown used to ducking their heads as they moved around slum offices in old warehouses suddenly found themselves sitting at concentric circles of desks under this magnificent rotunda! The headquarters were opened in October 1922 by the Prime Minister, Mr David Lloyd George.

Lord Devonport retired as Chairman in 1925 and during his term of office about £18,000,000 was committed for new construction and equipment and about £2,000,000 for river improvements. Not all this work had been completed when he withdrew, but already 80 acres of dock water and six miles of quays had been added. Completion of the dredging of the navigational channel took a few years longer, before the largest liners could reach the Royal Docks at high tide and vessels of 6,000 tons could get as far as the Pool, but the

Transit shed 1931. Between the two world wars, the industry was labour-intensive, with many small packages to be handled with the aid of hand-trucks and electric trolleys. This photograph shows South African oranges being discharged from the *Dunbar Castle* in 1931.

Fox Photos Limited

P.L.A. Warehouses. 1. Inspecting wool in bales at London Dock.

P.L.A. Collection, Museum of London

challenge of this formidable problem which had shadowed the port for centuries had at last been met. Much else had been achieved. The main dock at Tilbury had been enlarged from its original 74 acres to 90 acres and a great double-deck riverside cargo jetty had been built just above the dock entrance, connected to the shore by a curved railway approach viaduct. For several years before the war a practice had been growing of vessels calling in London for partial loading or discharge and then proceeding to Continental ports for partial loading or discharge there. The riverside cargo jetty was specifically designed for speedy and efficient service to such vessels. In the Royal Docks grain and meat-handling facilities were greatly improved. From the turn of the century, with the introduction and improvement of refrigeration equipment, the trade in frozen meat had been building up. A sorting shed and cold store was, therefore, built at the Royal Albert Dock immediately after the war, with conveyor belts to the quayside, at a cost of £400,000. Perhaps most significantly, London now provided the largest storage facilities in the country for petrol. The first such installation had been established well down-stream before the war, served by tankers of 12,000 tons. The P.L.A. decreed that they should approach no nearer to London than Thames Haven, but special craft were permitted to carry the products up the river. During the war and immediate post-war years there was a very rapid expansion of this activity at Thames Haven and at Purfleet.

As Lord Devonport left the scene, his programme almost completed, the future seemed promising. Britain had recovered from the war and was set for expansion: that was the general belief. What happened next is best indicated statistically. Between 1925 and 1931 the value of India's overseas trade was halved and the decline in trade with the Dominions was measured thus:

	Imports from 1925 (£ mlns) 1931		Exports to 1925 (£ mlns) 1931	
Australia	£72.6	£45.7	£60.2	£14.5
Canada	£70.6	£32.6	£27.6	£20.6
New Zealand	£51.3	£37.6	£23.1	£11.2
South Africa	£25.1	£13.1	£30.6	£21.9
Totals	£219.6	£129.0	£141.5	£ 68.2

Even by 1925 Britain's merchant fleet, although restored to its pre-war tonnage, represented only 32.1 per cent of the world total tonnage, compared with 44.2 per cent in 1915. Invisible earnings from shipping never again touched the 1914 peak. The British Empire's share of the world's carrying trade was below 40 per cent by 1931, compared with 47.5 per cent in 1912. United States and Japanese competition was becoming intense. Between the two world wars British exports never exceeded 84 per cent of the 1913 figures. By the early 1930s Britain's invisible exports were no longer sufficient to cover the deficit on the balance of trade.

Just as, in earlier prosperous times, the Port of London had been a barometer of Britain's fortunes, so now its activity reflected the slump. Practically all development of the port ceased between 1929 and 1936, but a few important plans were brought to fruition before the full effects of the crisis struck. On the south bank a new deep-water Quebec Dock was cut out and opened in 1926 and other improvements made in the Surrey Commercial

P.L.A. Warehouses. 2. A row of balances used to weigh silk.
P.L.A. Collection, Museum of London

P.L.A. Warehouses. 3. Nutmeg stored and displayed at London Dock.

group. In 1928 new timber sheds and discharging berths were provided at Lavender and Acorn Ponds to serve the softwood trade with Canada, Russia and Scandinavia. During the late 1920s new ship passages were cut to link the four docks in the West India-Millwall complex into one connected water space. In the East India Dock a new principal entrance lock was opened in 1931 and the transit sheds were extended and modernised.

The most ambitious work was at Tilbury. On 29th September, 1929 a new entrance lock was opened which could take the largest vessel afloat; it was 1,000 feet long, 100 feet wide and 45½ feet deep at high water. The depth of the main side docks was increased to 38 feet and a new dry dock was built which was the longest in the port (750 feet). On 16th May, 1930 a new passenger terminal was opened at Tilbury, built jointly by the P.L.A. and the London, Midland and Scottish Railway Company. This station connected directly with a Customs Hall, through which passengers proceeded to a floating landing stage to board liners sailing to India and the Far East.

With these improvements, the P.L.A. tightened its belt and took up a defensive position to weather the economic storm. It became more important to reduce port charges than further to improve facilities; in the decade ending 1936 rates were progressively cut by £1 million a year. Only in that year was further capital expenditure approved. The old jetties in the Royal Victoria Dock were then swept away and replaced by three-quarters of a mile of lineal deep-water quay, and the Ministry of Transport provided a new wide approach road, the two-miles-long Silvertown Way. The jetties had been a vaunted feature of the dock when first it was opened, but they were unsuitable for the economic spacing of the larger vessels which had now appeared and the substantial warehouses adjoining them which had been built to handle grain

108

and general cargoes had been turned over by 1930 to storage of tobacco. Now it was hoped to bring new activity to the dock; when the hopes took shape and the work was put in hand, there was no wide realisation that another war was close.

Between the two world wars the general pattern of activity in the port did not change fundamentally, though its volume declined. Tilbury, with its regular sailings to the Far East and Australia, handled a great deal of tea, rice, copra, fruit and dairy produce from that part of the world, a good deal of general and miscellaneous cargo, and a significant passenger traffic. In 1929 over 306,000 passengers passed through the port, but this included some who travelled in liners using the Royal Docks. The lines which used Tilbury regularly were P & O, Orient, Bibby, Clan, Ellerman, Harrison, Anchor, Brocklebank, East Asiatic, Horn, Rotterdam Lloyd and Scottish Shire Shipping. From 1927 a quay in the tidal basin was allocated for a nightly service to Dunkirk operated jointly by the L.M.S. Railway and the Angleterre-Lorraine-Alsace Steamship Company.

In the Royals, the Albert Dock became the headquarters of the trade in frozen meat, with concentration of this activity at the west end of the north quay, where there were refrigerated sorting sheds. One of them, at No 33 berth, had a capacity of a quarter of a million carcases and, taking the dock as a whole, it was not unusual for 280 insulated road vans and 90 insulated rail wagons to be loaded in an eight-hour shift. That meant handling, say, 14,500 quarters of chilled or frozen beef, 2,000 carcases of mutton and 2,000 packages of offal. Many leading shipping companies had their appropriated berths in the Royal Albert Dock, among them Shaw, Savill and Albion, the Atlantic Transport Company, Houlder Brothers, British India Steam

P.L.A. Warehouses. 4. Wine barrels outside the Crescent Wine Vaults at London Dock.
P.L.A. Collection, Museum of London

Field Marshal Bernard Montgomery seen addressing dockers at a critical moment during the Second World War.   *P.L.A. Collection, Museum of London*

Navigation, Lamport and Holt, Brocklebanks, P & O, the New Zealand Shipping Company, Nelson, the Messageries Maritimes de France, and Nippon Yusen Kaisha. The Victoria Dock handled mainly meat, wheat, tobacco, grain and a good deal of general cargo. The Royal Mail Line, Nippon Yusen Kaisha, and the Prince, Highland and Blue Star lines all had quay space regularly booked and their vessels entered from Galleons Reach, through the Royal Albert Dock. Regular users of the King George V Dock included Cunard, whose 35,655 ton *Mauretania* berthed there in 1939, White Star, P & O, Blue Funnel, Glen, Atlantic Transport and Commonwealth and Dominion.

The East India Docks were used by freight vessels of up to 7,000 tons, including the smaller Union Castle, Blue Star and Ellerman ships. The West India Docks demonstrated a link with their past, in that they still handled rum imports and more sugar and Caribbean hardwood than any other dock. They also had an important seasonal trade, from late October until the spring, in dried fruit.

A considerable proportion of the goods entering London and St Katharine Docks between the wars arrived in lighters which had loaded from vessels berthed in docks further down the river. The extensive storage facilities in their warehouses, conveniently close to the City, had come to be regarded and used as an extension of the modern dock facilities downstream. These docks remained the home of the tea, wool, wine and spirits trades; they handled coffee, rubber, ivory, gums and wax, perfume and essential spirits. Their remarkable staffs of specialists were still kept busy. Canned goods, seasonal dried fruit and veneers and plywood were also dealt with in their warehouses. Even in the 1930s the London-St Katharine complex earned itself the description of "the world's greatest concentration of portable wealth".

Finally, the Surrey Commercial Docks continued to concentrate on softwood and a significant portion of the American trade, particularly wheat and dairy produce. An immense number of lighters operated there, mainly handling timber, the sorting, piling, marking and storage of which was the responsibility of P.L.A. staff. Until well into the 1920s, some softwood and bulk grain cargoes continued to arrive in the Thames in square-rigged sailing vessels.

Then came another war, and this time the port was not to escape as lightly as in 1914-18. Before it was over, normal activities had been completely disrupted, much of the port equipment had been moved elsewhere, and damage assessed at £13½ millions had been caused to P.L.A. property. As shipping was diverted from London, its sea commerce was progressively reduced to about a quarter of the pre-war level. There was, however, no lack of purposeful activity. Throughout the war, the P.L.A. operated as a Port Emergency Committee, responsible to the Ministry of Transport for removal inland of stores of food and raw materials, for civil defence, fire-fighting and first aid, and for salvage and wreck-raising. In the opening months of the war the Thames estuary was besieged by magnetic mines. In the summer of 1940 river craft and P.L.A. staff were involved in the Dunkirk evacuation; 808 Thames lifeboats, large numbers of sailing barges, tugs and yachts, even a fire-float and a sludge-hopper, were drawn into this operation. In September 1940 began a fierce aerial attack which continued unabated for 57 consecutive nights. On Saturday, 7th September, 400 German aircraft arrived over the port and their bombs devastated every dock except Tilbury. Timber pounds in the Surrey Commercial complex blazed from end to end for a whole week. In this series of raids, seven of the West India sugar warehouses were destroyed and there were two direct hits on the P.L.A. headquarters, one of which destroyed the beautiful rotunda. A third of the warehouses and transit sheds in the port were destroyed or damaged and cargoes had to be stored in prefabricated huts or often simply under tarpaulins. Nearly a thousand high explosive and many thousands of incendiary bombs fell on the port and it became the most consistently and heavily bombed civilian target in the country.

A great deal of preparation for the D-Day invasion of the Continent in 1944 took place on the Thames. The "Pluto" pipeline through which fuel was supplied to the invading armies was fabricated there, as was a large proportion of the great prefabricated caissons which were towed across the Channel to make artificial harbours on the coast of Normandy. In the spring of 1944 Field

THE PORT OF LONDON

Marshal Bernard Montgomery told the 16,000 London dockers that the success or failure of the invasion would depend upon their efforts and later, as more than 300 ships and a thousand barges sailed down the river, dockers and their families were among crowds on every quay and pierside to cheer them as they passed. Fifty thousand soldiers, nine thousand vehicles and 80,000 tons of military supplies were carried in that first invasion fleet. Afterwards, between June 1944 and the end of the war, shipments to Europe from the Thames totalled two and three-quarter million tons of stores, including more than 200,000 vehicles.

Thus, as another century approached mid-term, the Port of London and its people were cast in a heroic role. They shared in an historic victory, and, in common with the whole British people, they emerged to a future of doubt and difficulty on an unprecedented scale.

A fierce aerial attack on the Port of London which began in September 1940 was maintained by the German Luftwaffe for 57 consecutive nights. This photograph shows the Surrey Docks ablaze. *P.L.A. Collection, Museum of London*

CHAPTER SIX

Reconstruction and Reassessment

IN BRITAIN, the years immediately following the Second World War were a strange period of heightened expectations, stimulated by victory in a titanic struggle, and yet of bleak austerity, reflecting the staggering cost of that struggle. A year after the armistice bread was still rationed; in 1947 there was a disastrous shortage of fuel; as late as 1951 butter was limited to three ounces for each person per week. Ration books did not disappear until 1954. During this same period many new, ambitious and expensive social and industrial policies were applied. Independence was granted to India, Pakistan, Burma and Ceylon and Britain subscribed to the objective of liberalisation of trade epitomised in the General Agreement on Tariffs and Trade (G.A.T.T.) signed in 1947. Not for many years was there full realisation of the extent to which Britain's position as a great trading nation operating at the centre of a Commonwealth economic community had been undermined by the war.

Until 1939 Britain had covered the cost of more than a third of her imports by so-called "invisible exports": income from overseas investments, income from shipping services (Britain owned over 26 per cent of world tonnage in 1939), income from insurance and other financial services provided by the City of London. By 1945 virtually the whole of the overseas investments had been sold, all the accumulated reserves of gold and silver had been used, a third of British merchant ships had been sunk or disabled, and exports (by volume) had dropped to 40 per cent of the pre-war level. Further, something like £16,000 millions had been borrowed — about half the total cost of the war to Britain — and heavy borrowing had to be continued into peace-time. These were grim realities.

For some years bulk purchase agreements and long-term contracts covered much U.K.-Commonwealth trade, and Australia, New Zealand and South Africa took most of their exports from Britain. But, as Britain's share of world export markets declined in the 1950s, Commonwealth countries rapidly developed their trade in other quarters. Between 1953 and 1962 total Commonwealth imports increased by 46 per cent, but their imports from the United Kingdom rose by only 12 per cent. Where once these countries had been best served by selling their primary products to Britain and buying British manufactures in exchange, there were now other customers available to them. A time came in the early 1960s when Australia was selling more wool

Viscount Waverley of Westdean, who was Chairman of the P.L.A. from 1946 to 1958.

Courtesy P.L.A.

to Japan, and Canada more wheat to Communist China, than to Britain. The Commonwealth was also developing its own manufacturing industries. Indian textiles began to threaten those of Lancashire. When India bought four steel mills from abroad, only one of them was supplied from Britain. The fact was that Britain no longer had the resources to assist fully the economic development of the newly-industrialising nations. She had not even the resources to ensure their continued defence; Australia and New Zealand signed a new defence pact with the United States, from which Britain was excluded. These countries, as well as Canada, were more open to American economic penetration than ever before. And South Africa, in 1961, chose to leave the Commonwealth altogether. As these trends developed, something equally significant was happening in Europe. More efficient, and generously subsidised, British agriculture and increased food imports from Europe reduced the U.K.'s dependence on the Commonwealth. Between 1959 and 1962, by which time a new pattern of world trade had clearly emerged, trade between the U.K. and Europe increased almost by half, bringing it level with trade with Commonwealth countries.

The economists caught up with events. They established that trade between relatively advanced countries had prospered most, and that other countries which were at approximately the same stage of development had successfully developed much closer trade links. It was upon this economic reality that six western European nations in 1957 based the European Economic Community, the so-called Common Market, to coordinate and stimulate their trade. For years Britain remained hesitant and uncertain about her new role. It was still possible to argue during the 'fifties that Britain's trading performance was satisfactory. The industrial revolution and expansion of world trade in the nineteenth century had given her such a head start over all competitors that it was inevitable that her share of the world market in manufactured goods must now decline. The two alarming features of the new situation were the failure to balance loss of exports to the Commonwealth with increased exports elsewhere, and a consistent inability to match the growth rate of every other major industrial country. There were restrictions upon capital investment by industry, industrial uncertainty and unrest, with the Port of London the scene of some of the most damaging strikes, and a general crisis of world confidence in sterling.

As throughout history, the fortunes of the Port of London mirrored the fortunes of the country of which it was the heart. The decline in Commonwealth trade eroded the base upon which the port had developed. The emergence of the E.E.C. as a powerful new trading bloc changed the pattern of cargo movements and Continental ports emerged as potentially dangerous rivals; in 1945 Rotterdam was behind London in tonnage handled, in 1955 it moved ahead, and by 1969 it was handling three times as much traffic as London.

Sir Leslie Ford, Chief Executive of the P.L.A. from 1948 to 1964.   *Courtesy P.L.A.*

During this period the port industry everywhere was undergoing a techno-logical revolution. New types of vessels, new methods of packaging cargoes, and new quayside equipment created, in time, a basic new concept of through freight traffic from supplier to customer without intermediate man-handling. One of the consequences of that was a collapse of the elaborate warehousing and marketing services which had been traditionally supplied in London.

When the war ended, however, the tasks of immediate reconstruction absorbed all the energies and resources available. If anything was discerned of the more complex problems ahead, the P.L.A., like the archetypal Cockney who whistles his way through adversity, showed no sign of dismay. In 1946 it re-established the annual wool auctions on pre-war lines. In the summer of 1948, it resumed river and docks cruises and in that year 22,000 sight-seers sailed through the port. Trade came back in a rush and very soon the port was loaded beyond its capacity. By 1947 the total tonnage of goods handled directly by the P.L.A. was the highest since 1921, if one excepts the special military traffic of 1945. By 1952 the tonnage passing through the port exceeded anything previously recorded. By 1954 the tonnage of shipping arriving in the river was an all-time record.

116

The port was under new leadership. Sir John Anderson, later Viscount Waverley of Westdean, became Chairman of the P.L.A. in January 1946. He had had a distinguished career in public service and in government and, at the age of sixty-three, was a national figure with a magisterial — if not imperial — cast of personality, with great resolution and quite unusual ability. His mind encompassed not only the broad sweep of policy-making, but also finer points of detail. Checking through the arrangements on the occasion of a royal visit to the docks, he was told that umbrellas would be available in case it should rain. The thought displeased him. "It will not rain," he pronounced, and nor did it, though there were downpours on the days preceding and following the event. Thereafter Anderson was known to some of his staff as "Jehovah" and there were many others who thought this description appropriate. His actual qualifications were those acquired as Governor of Bengal, as Home Secretary during the early difficult phase of the war, giving his name to the Anderson Shelter, and as Chancellor of the Exchequer.

In 1947 Anderson set up two committees to consider how best to avoid delays in the turn-round of shipping; one with shipowners and port employers, the other with master lightermen and barge-owners, with the trade unions represented on both. The following year he appointed Mr Leslie E. Ford, later Sir Leslie, to supervise the reconstruction programme. Ford had had a long and successful career in the industry and for the following fifteen years, as General Manager of the P.L.A., he guided the port through one of the most difficult periods of its history. Ford was well aware that major changes in the handling of cargo were on the way and he wasted no time in starting discussions with P.L.A. customers, ship-owners, manufacturers, wharfingers, the Customs and the trade unions.

First, however, the repair of wartime damage had to be completed. Quite half of the total storage accommodation in the docks had been destroyed and much of the equipment had been dispersed or damaged. Full restoration took a period of ten years. Work was always behind schedule, not for want of effort, nor even because of financial restriction, but because materials, particularly steel, were in short supply and heavy demand. Much improvisation was called for; it was a period of getting what one could where one could. The P.L.A. bought two large floating cranes from the government, a 30-ton floating derrick from the Admiralty, and 33 second-hand diesel mobile cranes elsewhere. An order for fifty 3-ton electric quay cranes placed within months of the armistice was not completed until three years later. In 1948 and 1950 a total of 112 more were ordered and the last of these was not operational until 1955.

Generally, the port was rebuilt in its pre-war image. Parts of St Katharine Dock had been so heavily bombed that no effort was made to reconstruct them, and some other historic parts of the port were also abandoned. The East

India Import Dock at Millwall had been dried out during the war and used for the construction of the caissons which formed the invasion harbours on the Normandy coast; soon after the war the Export Dock was filled in and sold and in 1947 work began on a Brunswick Wharf Power Station, which today dominates a stretch of the Thames which was once the scene of East India Company activity. In the other docks every effort was made to restore full trading activity as quickly as possible.

An absolute priority had to be given, of course, to clearing and improving the navigational channel into the port: the task, quite literally, of opening up the Thames again to the outside world. So many wrecks and other obstacles had accumulated in or near the channels used by shipping that it took a full five years to clear them. It had been impossible during the war to maintain a full programme of dredging, and a colossal backlog of work had built up. In the first two years three million cubic yards of silt were dredged from the enclosed docks, and an additional one and three-quarter million cubic yards from the river. Dredging continued year after year; it has always been, and remains, a permanent feature of port maintenance. At first, the mud and silt were carried out to sea and dumped beyond the estuary, but from 1960 new techniques made it possible to pump the spoil ashore on to marshland at Rainham. Millions of tons were removed from the river in this way, until the level of an area exceeding 200 acres had been raised by twelve to fifteen feet.

It was the responsibility of the P.L.A. to maintain not only a clear river, but also a clean one. A severe drought in 1949 which reduced the flow of fresh water coming over Teddington Weir from the upper Thames convinced everyone—and not least the nation's legislators at Westminster, beside whose debating chambers the river flowed—that pollution had built up to an

Every berth occupied in the Royal Albert Dock in 1958 as the port reached a peak of activity.
P.L.A. Collection, Museum of London

During the 1950s the P.L.A. railway system was improved and extended, but road haulage was providing intense competition. In this 1957 photograph exports are seen arriving at the **Royal Albert Dock** for shipment by rail and road.

P.L.A. Collection, Museum of London

appalling degree. The water was as black as ink. Anyone unfortunate enough to fall into it had to be rushed to hospital to be pumped clean. Rubbish thrown into the stream at London Bridge took an average of six weeks to reach the estuary; on one tide it travelled eight and a half miles downstream, but the next tide brought it back eight miles. Quite apart from the special circumstances of drought, the increased flow of domestic sewage and of industrial effluents, the raising of water temperature by discharges from many more riverside power stations and the greater draw-off of water from the upper Thames to supply London's needs had all combined to create a permanent and pungent problem. The oxygen content of the water fell to zero and sulphur compounds—the main pollutants—reacted to form hydrogen sulphide, popularly called "rotten eggs gas". A committee set up by the P.L.A. reported in 1954: "Samples taken now indicate at times a state of complete deoxygenation from Erith as far up-river as Battersea". In other words, the Thames was ecologically dead, and so it remained through most of the 'fifties. A 400-feet tidal model of the river between Teddington and Southend was built for the P.L.A. in 1952 and installed in a shed in the Royal Victoria Dock; with it experts were able to simulate all the complicated movements of the tides and flows, and thus were able to devise effective remedial measures. By the 'sixties the problem had been solved. Improvements were made at the great sewage treatment plants at Beckton and Crossness. In 1964 the P.L.A. acquired, and began to use, powers to control discharges into the Thames and in that year, for the first time since 1921, the oxygen content was maintained at a minimum five per cent in the hottest weather. By 1966 the Authority was able to report: "For the third year in succession no samples of river water were found to be wholly devoid of dissolved oxygen and in the autumn frequent reports were made of fish where none had been found for many years." A year later sea fish were reported in considerable numbers and variety five miles upstream of Gravesend, and by 1973 seventy-three species of fish had been counted in the river. In April 1974 the P.L.A. handed over most of its pollution control powers to the newly-constituted Thames Water Authority, and annual reports since then have shown continuing improvement.

Once dredging was well in hand, and the problem of pollution had been faced, a longer-term programme of improvements was prepared. The seaward limit of the Port of London was at No 1 Sea Reach buoy, following a line between Foulness to the north and Sheppey to the south. The statutory responsibility of the P.L.A. was to keep the channel from this point as far west as Gravesend dredged to a depth of 30 feet at low water, over a width of 1,000 feet. In fact, such a channel was restored as far as Coldharbour Point, about 33 miles from the seaward limit. From there to the entrance to the King George V dock — about seven miles — a 27-foot channel of 600 feet width was maintained; for the remaining ten miles to London Bridge there was a gradual narrowing of the channel, which also lost depth. In practical terms, it enabled vessels up to 10,000 grt* to reach the Upper Pool.

The launching of much larger vessels after the war created entirely new problems, particularly the arrival of big oil tankers to discharge at jetties in the river. Over a thousand ships entered or left the Thames every week and the movement among them of these tankers presented a real challenge. When under way, they could take a mile to stop, even with engines put full astern. When berthing, they needed to turn in the river. When arriving in the estuary, their draught left only a couple of feet between their bottoms and the sea bed. As channels and banks constantly change their formations, there was a need for more regular and detailed hydrographic surveys, and it became desirable to provide a deeper, straighter and more stable main channel as an approach to the port.

Since 1795 the British Admiralty had been charting the waters of the globe; knowledge of the Thames and its estuary in 1945 still owed a great deal to the efforts more than a century earlier of a Lieutenant, Bullock, who had supervised the Admiralty survey of this area. The Second World War hastened the development of new equipment for survey work and in 1948 the Hydrographic Department of the Admiralty began a new survey. The echo-sounder had replaced the lead-line and radio and electronic position-fixing had ended earlier dependence upon purely visual objects when taking bearings. The P.L.A. commissioned a special Admiralty survey of the esturarial approaches to the Thames and, at about the same time, it equipped the Hydrographic Section of its own River Department with echo-sounders and began a new survey of the river within the port limits. After 1964, the

*grt = gross register tonnage.

The Operations Room of the Thames Navigation Service, set up at Gravesend in 1959.

Courtesy P.L.A.

P.L.A. was responsible for the whole area, as an Act of Parliament in that year extended the boundaries of the port 22 miles eastward of the earlier limit at No 1 Sea Reach buoy, to take in the estuary.

In May 1959 the P.L.A. established a Thames Navigation Service, with its headquarters at Gravesend. Using radar, radio-telephony, automatic tide gauges and patrol vessels, the T.N.S. quickly established itself as the nerve-centre controlling all shipping movements. In the early years, its radar displays covered the river from Tilbury to Southend, but coverage was steadily expanded until, with the opening of a new station at Warden Point in the Isle of Sheppey in 1973, constant surveillance was established over the whole area from the port limits in the North Sea to the upper docks in the river. Tidal information, including early warning of any surges, is obtained by radio telemetry from a series of automatic gauges, including two installed as far away as Walton-on-the-Naze and Margate. Their accuracy is such that Gravesend is able to monitor deviations from the predicted heights of tides of as little as 40 mm. This information makes possible precise assessment of depths in the approach channels to the port.

The T.N.S. headquarters is manned throughout the 24 hours and every thirty minutes it transmits a radio bulletin on the general situation in the port, giving details of weather, visibility, tidal variations and the positions of dredgers, works and obstructions. It can also maintain direct radio contact with individual vessels. When it was first established only about five per cent of vessels were equipped with V.H.F. radio, but the proportion increased each year until, by March 1969, the P.L.A. felt able to apply to all vessels in the river, for the first time, a series of "general directions". These require vessels to give advance notice of their arrival and departure, to comply with a specific movement programme, including approach by a designated channel, and to use prescribed anchorages. This is called "aided routeing" and inside the port limits it has supplanted navigation according to the age-old traditions of the sea. Today the Thames Navigation Service Operations Room helps to co-ordinate the work of pilots, the Port Health Authority, H.M. Customs, the police and the fire brigade. It provides a minute-by-minute flow of information to ship-owners, masters, pilots, tug operators, dock and berthing masters. With its sophisticated electronic aids, backed by a fleet of patrol launches, it has become the safest navigation service in the world.

One other major development was required before the big new oil tankers could reach the Thames safely. The main approach to the port had been by the Edinburgh Channels, but a deeper and straighter channel was necessary. The P.L.A. dredged one and a quarter million cubic yards of spoil from the sea-bed to create the Knock John Channel as a second deep-water approach. When this was opened in June 1967 it provided a minimum 48 feet depth at every high tide, over a width of 1,200 feet.

Before the Knock John Channel was opened, the largest tanker to have entered the port was the *Seven Skies*, 93,250 dwt* and 857 feet long. In October 1968, through the new channel, came the *Megara*, 206,000 dwt and 1,066 feet long. The popular press made much of the fact that her crew used bicycles to move around her deck. Later came the *Romeo Maersk*, 290,000 tons and 1,140 feet long. Even in a channel with 48 feet depth, vessels of this size must be manoeuvred within critical margins. The responsibility for bringing them safely to port is shared by their masters and the pilots of the Corporation of Trinity House, who still exercise the exclusive right — granted by Henry VIII in 1514 — to bring sea-going vessels up the river. There are 500 London pilots, licensed by Trinity House, but all self-employed and pooling and sharing their fees.

If a tanker has come up-Channel, she is joined by a pilot as she passes Folkestone; if from the north, the pilot comes aboard off Harwich. From these points, speed and timing are of great importance. The shallower patches in the approach channels must be navigated when the tide is at the right level. The Thames Navigation Service keeps the pilot informed how the tide is making: whether there is any tendency for it to be below predicted height or for high water to be behind schedule. The pilot advises the master when he considers it is safe to enter and what course to follow. In Sea Reach, where land begins to close in on either side, a Harbour Service launch joins the tanker and leads her in, ensuring an uninterrupted passage. Well before she approaches the jetty where she is to berth, tugs are in attendance; one passes a

---

*dwt = deadweight tons.

Before international air traffic developed, Tilbury was a busy passenger port. An Ocean Passenger Terminal was opened in 1957, but by then the traffic was already declining. In this photograph four P & O liners are seen berthed close together at Tilbury: *Himalaya, Strathaird, Strathnaver* and *Chitral.* *Courtesy P & O Group*

line into her stern and another a line into her bows and they swing her round in the river to face the last of the flood tide. During this operation a brilliant light flashes at the top of a high pylon: the Tanker Traffic Warning Light, operated by the T.N.S. at Gravesend. Once round, the tanker should be fairly close to the berth. A boat comes out and takes lines ashore and, as these are secured, the tugs let go of their lines and move round to push on the beam of the vessel to edge her alongside.

The oil super-tanker is probably the most spectacular form of mechanised bulk transport of cargo by sea, but its appearance during the late 'fifties and early 'sixties was part of an overall trend towards larger vessels and simplified cargo handling techniques. The new management sciences being formulated at that time postulated minimum stocks and quick turn-over as the route to maximum profit. The conventional wisdom was that cargo vessels spent half their time in port, discharging or loading. Money was also tied up in warehousing and market management. If these delays, and consequent expense, could be avoided, everyone was expected to benefit. The new vessels were initially expensive, but they were larger and faster and so fewer would be required. The ports, however, would have to be re-organised and mechanised so that they could achieve 24-hour turn-round of vessels. In order to do that, cargoes would need to be consigned in larger and more uniform packages. As an increasing proportion of cargoes was on U.K.-Europe routes, these could be carried directly on lorries, by cross-Channel ferry, from supplier to inland supermarket or warehouse.

In fact, a vast range of cargoes were handled in the traditional way for about twenty years after the war ended in 1945. Those first affected by change were oil and wine, wheat and sugar, all of which could be readily handled in bulk by mechanical means. Oil set the pattern. Petroleum traffic through the Port of London began as early as 1862, only three years after the first well was drilled, in Pennsylvania. The 110-foot brig *Elizabeth Watts* arrived in the Victoria Dock in that year with 901 barrels of rock oil and 428 barrels of coal oil from Philadelphia. By 1864 London was importing 140,000 tons of oil a year. Legislation in 1871 established Thames Haven as the point beyond which vessels carrying low flashpoint petroleum should not pass and a petroleum wharf was built there soon afterwards. Others followed and by 1914 there were three petroleum jetties on the river and 75 storage tanks beside it, with a total capacity of 300,000 tons. During the First World War, Shell established the first Thames refinery, but the explosive growth of the industry came after the Second World War. Other refineries were established then by the Mobil Oil Company at Coryton, by the Occidental Company on Canvey Island and by

Lighters were once much more numerous in the port and this was a typical scene. Paper pulp imports are seen being discharged into a lighter in the Royal Victoria Dock.

Courtesy P.L.A.

British Petroleum on the Isle of Grain — the latter not strictly within the Port of London, as it fronts the Medway, but served by the shipping lanes of the Thames Estuary. By the middle 1970s these refineries, between them, had developed a capacity to handle well over 30 million tons a year. The biggest of several storage depots, that at Thames Haven, has a capacity of two million tons. By 1970 petroleum traffic represented almost half of the total tonnage through the port (28.9 million tonnes,* of a total of 59.5 millions), and from that date the Thames has received a regular procession of super-tankers, drawing up to 45 feet. It is a far cry from the pre-war traffic, when the average size of tankers was 12,000 dwt. The construction of the refineries close to the consuming market was a direct outcome of the development of the giant tankers; previously the policy had been to import refined products.

Looked at unemotionally, as businessmen do, wine can be handled in much the same way as oil. So, by the late 1950s the wine trade was contemplating the possibility of shipment in larger, more economical containers than the traditional casks. The first experiments were made with 500-gallon tanks of stainless steel or plastic, which could be lifted on and off ship by crane. After that, general cargo vessels were equipped with built-in tanks of much greater capacity and with associated pumping equipment. From that, it was a short step to the purpose-built wine tanker which was berthing regularly in London Dock by the early 'sixties and discharging up to 12,000 gallons each time. A new quay was built there, with intake pipes and glass-lined tanks to store 200,000 gallons. Within a year this capacity had been almost trebled, and later it was increased to 800,000 gallons. The British taste for wine was developing fast. In 1969 the P.L.A. transferred the Bulk Wine Terminal to the former Wood Wharf in the West India Dock, installed there a vast array of vats made of glass-fibre which could hold two million gallons, and thus established London as the leading port in this trade. The terminal was soon handling three times the volume of wine that had been shipped to London before the war. And it was not only wine; in 1976 a tanker made the first bulk delivery of rum — 300,000 gallons, worth £11 millions at retail prices, surely one of the most valuable cargoes of all times. It was discharged, as wine regularly is, into road tankers, four at a time. A large open space behind the 700 feet of quay was specifically designed for such handling, to enable rapid delivery to customers' wine vaults. Pumps can fill a 4,300-gallon tanker in about 45 minutes. The whole terminal constitutes bonded premises and H.M. Customs are closely involved in the daily running of the place.

The first dry cargo to be handled in bulk was grain. As mentioned in an earlier chapter, the Central Granary built in Millwall Dock in 1902-3 replaced bucket or skip discharge by pneumatic tubes. This had been a marvel of its time, but by the 1960s it was not able to compete with new installations in Rotterdam and Antwerp. A good deal of traffic was being lost to London and

*(1 metric tonne = 0.984 tons).

Fork-lift trucks operating in large modern transit sheds became the post-war pattern for conventional break-bulk cargoes. The photograph shows "F" Shed in Millwall Dock in 1964.

P.L.A. Collection, Museum of London

so, in 1965, the P.L.A. secured government approval of a scheme to build a new Bulk Grain Terminal on the riverside at Tilbury, just outside the docks complex. It was completed and operational by June 1969, at a cost of £5 millions. Beside a 950-foot jetty in the river, the water was dredged to a depth of 45 feet, so that ships of up to 77,000 dwt can berth at any state of the tide. From the jetty two 180-foot towers rise above the water, each equipped with a flexible system of bucket elevators with which to lift the grain from ships' holds. Two pneumatic hoses supplement these elevators, reaching into corners and other inaccessible places. The two towers, which were modelled on Canadian practice, give an appreciably higher rate of discharge than any other European terminal, at 2,000 tons an hour. When the grain has been lifted from the ship, it travels on conveyor belts to three silos, grouped in a single structure 127 feet high and with a total storage capacity of 106,000 tons. Alternatively, the grain can be delivered into barges, coasters, rail vans or lorries, or directly to three privately-operated mills and a new starch products installation which have developed alongside the terminal. With the opening of this new complex, the Central Granary which had for so long dominated the Millwall skyline was demolished in 1970. The success of Tilbury in winning back and holding a good share of grain shipments to Europe is shown by the average annual throughput of 1,586,000 tons, to the end of 1977, with a peak of 1,780,000 tons in 1972.

For a century and a half the great sugar warehouses of the West India Dock were one of the outstanding architectural features of the port. Originally, sugar arrived in them in oak casks, and then later in jute bags. Some of the warehouses were destroyed in the war and in 1949 an experiment took place in bulk shipment of sugar. Over 5,000 tons was unloaded with grab cranes into lighters and taken directly to the refineries at Silvertown and Plaistow. By 1965 the discharge of bags of sugar on to the North Quay of the West India Import Dock had ended for ever. A new deep-water jetty was built by Tate and Lyle in

Woolwich Reach in 1967, able to berth much larger vessels carrying up to 15,000 tons, and activities were concentrated there. Grab cranes now discharge into a conveyor trough, which delivers into this refinery, which processes almost half the total U.K. consumption of sugar.

We have identified and traced through to full realisation some of the new techniques of freight handling developed after 1945. Now we must go back to the immediate post-war years to examine how problems associated with other types of cargo were faced. At the heart of the new thinking at that time was the electric forklift truck, together with the pallets on which loads were stacked and carried. From 1950 these trucks and their associated equipment were purchased in increasing numbers each year. In 1951, with the agreement of the unions, a pilot scheme was operated at a specially-designed loading berth in the West India Dock, and the speed of ship loading was increased by more than 20 per cent. The number of man-handling operations was reduced from five to two. This experiment was pronounced a success, similar handling methods were introduced in the Royal Docks and in the Surrey Commercial system, and later in all the others. Leslie Ford summarised the achievement: "A new rhythm of mechanised cargo handling began to take the place of methods conceived in an age of unlimited manual labour." At the time there were over 30,000 workers employed in the port.

In order that the forklift trucks and their palletised loads could move freely and quickly, quays were widened and re-surfaced and transit sheds were reconstructed with larger doors and higher roofs. During the same period, a programme of new sheds, new roads, new dock gates and new canteens was carried through. In accordance with the recommendations of a Ports Efficiency

Not until the coming of the containers did the port work round the clock, but ships at their berths in the King George V Dock during an earlier period made a striking spectacle.

P.L.A. Collection, Museum of London

Committee appointed by the government in 1952, the P.L.A. concentrated on the reconstruction of thirteen specific berths in various docks; one was completed in 1953 and seven more by 1955, by which time it became possible in the King George V Dock to reintroduce the pre-war practice of allocating berths to ship-owners on a permanent basis. The cost of capital investment increased year by year, from a modest £128,000 in 1948 to a peak of £1,842,000 in 1957. That was the year in which the Authority's capital reserves were exhausted, so that thereafter investment had to be financed by borrowing. By the time the P.L.A. celebrated its fiftieth anniversary in 1959, post-war investment totalled just under £11¼ millions and the total since the Authority's inception in 1909 was just under £30 millions.

The Port of London was one of the first major industrial undertakings to confront the special problems which arise from the pace of technological innovation. Correct timing can be crucial when a major investment is being made, but sometimes it is a matter of luck rather than judgement. To delay with re-equipment can mean missing market opportunities; to proceed too quickly can involve early obsolescence and give significant advantage to competitors who delay investment until more productive technology has been developed. With hindsight, it is possible to see that not all the P.L.A. investment was justified by events. Possibly the extensive repairs to the Central Granary at Millwall and the purchase of two floating grain elevators paid off during the twenty years before they were swept away in favour of a new Bulk Grain Terminal at Tilbury. But the investment in bringing an extensive P.L.A. railway system back to full efficiency can hardly have been cost-effective. During the 1950s rail track throughout the Royals group was renewed, sidings were extended on the north side of the Royal Victoria Dock, 21 diesel-electric locomotives were ordered to replace steam, and a new locomotive repair shed was authorised. While this was happening, evidence was accumulating of a significant switch from rail to road by those who were sending goods to, or collecting from, the docks. Rail traffic declined rapidly; road haulage carried 2 million tons in 1947, 2½ million tons in 1948, 3 million tons in 1951, 4 million tons in 1958 and was moving up towards 5 million tons by 1965. By the late 'sixties almost all the rail tracks had disappeared and the locomotives were being sold off.

A major investment at Tilbury was also of doubtful wisdom, though it seemed sensible at the moment of decision. The P & O and Orient Lines had announced their intention to introduce new vessels which would call at Tilbury, where already about 150,000 passengers a year were passing through. Air competition had scarcely begun to present a challenge and the P.L.A. saw a prospect of expanding business. A new Ocean Passenger Terminal was conceived and constructed on a lavish scale: a reception hall decorated with striking black-and-white murals and with banking, communications and refreshment facilities, a viewing gallery for visitors, a baggage hall, and a 100,000 square feet transit shed. Boat trains ran from St Pancras station and for those who came by car, there was parking for 700 vehicles. The whole complex cost £1,590,000. Viscount Waverley sounded a note of uncertainty in his speech at the opening ceremony in 1957: "In designing this extension we made the best estimate we could of the developing requirements of the great ships that now use this port. It must necessarily rest with others to take advantage of the facilities provided . . . We have performed this act of faith and we hope for the helpful understanding and collaboration of all concerned."

The P.L.A. never adopted a cautious posture of "wait-and-see", and had it done so it would almost certainly have fared much worse. History has confirmed the wisdom of the great majority of its decisions. A good example of its bold progressive approach was the way in which the Royal Victoria Dock was brought up to a standard which made it the best-equipped in the world. Tobacco remained an important cargo there, with P.L.A. staff performing many technical operations for the importers who used the Authority's warehouses. Chilled meat from South America was discharged mechanically at berths in which £650,000 was invested. There were special sheds for green fruit and vegetables, and a bulk grain depot on the south side of the dock. At the end of the decade, the largest transit shed in the whole port was brought into use at No 4 berth, serving the United States Lines. It could handle cargoes of two ships simultaneously and was considered a model of the new kind of shed required for mechanical handling; it had 140,000 square feet of clear space and a 50-foot canopy over loading platforms at each end for road haulage vehicles.

So the Port of London Authority came to its jubilee year. It could look back over many troubled times, there was a question-mark as big as a rainbow over this and most other ports, but all-in-all the future seemed promising. Over a thousand vessels were entering or leaving the Thames each week; their net registered tonnage totalled nearly 80.5 millions in the fiftieth anniversary year, which was well over double that handled in the first year of the Authority's existence. The river had been cleared and dredged and a serious start had been made on cleaning it up. The docks had been rebuilt and re-equipped. Ships and cargoes were being handled at almost every berth every day. Over fifty large vessels could usually be seen at any time in the Royal Docks alone.

The pattern of port activity had not changed greatly. The West India Docks still handled the general trade of the West Indies and the Caribbean, although, additionally, it took vessels trading with most other ports of the world. Rum still arrived there and was lightered to the vaults in London Dock; the hardwood trade was still centred on the Wood Wharf. The Surrey Commercial group of docks still handled virtually the whole of the softwood

Tankers bringing crude oil to the great Thames refineries have steadily increased in size. This 1974 photograph shows the *Melania*, 212,750 dwt, discharging at B jetty at Shell Haven.

Shell photograph

cargoes, through fifty great post-war sheds, but mobile cranes and new storage methods had eliminated the traditional man-handling of planks by the deal porters. Millwall still concentrated on handling bulk grain, though Persian Gulf export traffic and Scandinavian trade was also directed over its berths. The Royals was a centre for the meat and fruit trade. The Albert Dock provided accommodation for 500,000 carcases and had a mechanical berth to discharge bananas at the rate of 80,000 stems a day. The warehouses of London Dock and Cutler Street were still, in 1959, a great emporium of the most valuable cargoes passing through the port: wines and spirits, cigars, tea, carpets, watches and clocks, cameras and musical instruments, drugs, spices and perfumes, silks, rayons and nylons, and much else. Cutler Street handled a vast variety of general goods and its activities were not restricted to storage. Every week its delivery vans carried nearly four thousand samples of goods in stock to potential purchasers in the City and West End.

Activity on the river was still intense. About seven thousand lighters still moved between the docks, the wharves, and the warehouses. Pleasure steamers still sailed each morning from Tower Pier with day trippers seeking the excitement of Southend and Clacton. The private wharfingers were doing good business; the Hays Wharf group in the Pool of London, for example, could still claim proudly that it provided "the larder of London". Along the industrialised section of the river, the factories, the refineries, the power stations, the paper mills and the cement works were working to full capacity.

There seemed much to celebrate when, on 12th May, 1959, the Board of the P.L.A. sat down to lunch with Queen Elizabeth and the Duke of

Edinburgh, whose Coronation Cavalcade six years earlier had provided the most colourful Thames water pageant since the coronation of Anne Boleyn. Afterwards the royal party toured the London and Royal docks. Lord Waverley, who had presided over the great task of reconstruction, did not live to enjoy this occasion and he had been succeeded as Chairman of the P.L.A. by a distinguished ship-owner, Viscount Simon.

To a degree which no-one present could possibly have understood, that time was a watershed in British history. Recognition of the change in national fortunes since the war had at last dawned, a fundamental reassessment of Britain's place in the new international economic community was beginning and the necessary psychological, political and financial adjustments had still to be faced. Coincidentally, it was the time when new technology was beginning a revolution in cargo handling. The fiftieth annual report of the P.L.A. recorded that redevelopment of the port had been slowed down while a reappraisal was made. It stated that imports handled by the Authority had declined by ten per cent and that there had been a pronounced decline in the tonnage of goods offered to the Authority for warehousing. But the most pregnant passage in the report was buried in the detailed description of operations in the Royal Victoria Dock. "Improvements have been carried out at No 4 berth," it read, "to provide facilities for a continental container service."

It was the first time a P.L.A. annual report had mentioned the container.

The Grain Terminal at Tilbury was completed in 1969 and can discharge up to 2,000 tons an hour. *Photograph by Douglas Brown*

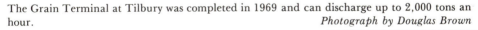

CHAPTER SEVEN

Containers: Tilbury Sets The Pace

IN THE drowsy mid-afternoon hours of a summer Sunday, news came that
a 32,000-ton United States Lines vessel, the *American Lancer*, had entered
the Thames Estuary. When she came alongside No 40 berth in Tilbury Docks
at 5.15 p.m. a rapidly-summoned team of fiteen dockers was waiting to
discharge her. On the next tide, only thirteen hours later, the vessel sailed
again, having discharged her U.K. cargo and reloaded.

In those thirteen hours history was made. The *American Lancer*, the first
trans-Atlantic container ship, was the harbinger of the most dramatic and
rapid transformation the port has ever known. Her cargo was carried entirely
in metal boxes, each measuring 8 × 8 × 20 feet and containing ten tons. Two
hundred of these were off-loaded and 320 others placed on board by two teams
of fifteen men and an expensive array of new equipment in the course of a
single night. Had the cargo been handled in the traditional "break-bulk"
manner, it would have taken 176 men—96 on the ship and 80 on the quay—
four or five days to achieve the same result. Not the least remarkable feature of
this performance was the availability of the men at the time they were
required. The London docker had always worked a regular 8 a.m. to 5 p.m.
shift five days a week and had rarely welcomed week-end overtime. And this
was not even an ordinary week-end: it was the Sunday night of the Whitsun
bank holiday week-end, a time when every industrial activity, except the
essential public services, was at a standstill. London thus became the first port
in the United Kingdom to offer facilities to ocean-going container ships and
established a head-start over any European rival port. The date was 2nd June,
1968.

The container, which has revolutionised the transport of freight, was not
in itself a revolutionary concept. From time immemorial, all cargoes were
carried in containers of one sort or another; the wooden cask and the tea chest
were containers. During the 1930s railways in Britain regularly moved suitable
freight—including ten thousand household removals each year—in large
containers which were transferred by crane between road vehicles and rail
"flats". In 1950 the Anglo-American Council of Productivity sent a team to the
United States to see what might be learnt there about improved methods of
cargo handling. Its report contained a short section on containers, concluding:

"While in Britain there is an appreciable and growing use of freight containers capable of being transferred by means of cranes between road and rail vehicles with, among other advantages, the avoidance of intermediate handling of individual packages and saving of packing, containers are not used to the same extent in America."

The attention of this investigative team was evidently not directed to the activities of the United States Army, for in the immediate post-war years it was busily experimenting with the packaging of freight in units of standard size, including containers, and with the development of container-carrying vehicles which could be driven on and off ships — what later became known as RO/RO (roll-on, roll-off) traffic. The U.S. Army established that 42 per cent of the total volume of the equipment and stores it needed to ship overseas *could* be containerised. In 1955 a study was made of all cargo passing through the Port of New York and this showed that about a third of all general cargo exports might be containerised. One or two American shipping companies thereupon carried a few containers experimentally as deck cargo and later proceeded to convert cargo ships into specialised container ships. By the late 1950s there was a widespread conviction that this was the future method for most cargo transport and a new kind of "cellular" vessel was being designed, terminals were being laid out and suitable handling machinery was being installed.

Initially, the scale of the problems was intimidating. Cellular ships could only be built when there was general agreement about standard dimensions for containers. Container berths required open space and lifting facilities of an entirely different kind from what existed. The speed of cargo movement over berths which became possible — and indeed was essential if the big capital expenditures were to be justified — called for new methods of documentation and control. Customs procedures needed to be drastically adjusted. Further, these changes had to be made internationally before the new techniques could be applied to ocean traffic. Consequently, the early development of container traffic took place in the United States only on road, rail and coastal shipping routes within the country.

As early as 1956 over five hundred loaded lorries crossed the English Channel, providing door-to-door freight service, and the number increased rapidly to reach 17,000 by 1963. During the 'sixties the emphasis moved to standard containers, the controversial "juggernauts" became familiar on British roads, British Rail developed the concept of the Freightliner express train carrying containers, and East Coast ports such as Felixstowe and Dover equipped themselves to attract RO/RO traffic. The P.L.A.'s thinking had always been to take account of ocean-going, as well as cross-Channel, shipping and this made its task more complex; in thought and action, however, it kept itself in the vanguard and Sir Leslie Ford kept closely in touch with all that was happening in the United States.

The concept of through transport from producer to customer developed rapidly after the Second World War and RO/RO vehicles were designed to carry unitised loads.

Courtesy P.L.A.

In March 1961 the government asked a committee headed by Viscount Rochdale "to consider to what extent the major docks and harbours of Great Britain are adequate to meet present and future national needs, whether the methods of working can be improved, and to make recommendations". This Committee reported that changes which had occurred in the patterns of trade were likely to favour ports on the east and south-east coasts of England, and one of its main recommendations was that most of the new investment in the industry over the following ten to fifteen years should be directed to development of Tilbury, Teesport, Leith and Southampton. The Committee said specifically that port facilities on the Thames should be expanded away from the centre of London, and it favoured Tilbury. It drew attention, also, to possible advantages to be gained by closing down the London and St Katharine Docks.

Most of the Rochdale conclusions were in line with plans already formulated by the P.L.A. Well before the Committee reported, the Authority's report for the year to March 1962 had stated: "The Authority was faced with new problems: the changing pattern of trade resulting from the possibility of the U.K.'s entry into the E.E.C., the prospect of a Channel link, either by bridge or tunnel, and of rapid changes in methods of cargo handling and packing and in the design of vessels. Large schemes of modernisation and development have been undertaken by the near Continental ports in the post-war period and these constitute a challenge—particularly to the port's trans-shipment traffic—which London must meet . . . The majority of the Authority's docks and quays were constructed before 1914 . . . The Authority, therefore, decided to embark on a modernisation and development programme, to be completed in six or seven years, at an estimated cost of some £30 millions. Such a programme must inevitably be preceded by a period of planning, but the next year or two should see a considerable acceleration in the rate of expenditure on work of a capital nature."

The planning and preparatory work was performed in the spirit of the latest management efficiency theories of the day. The P.L.A. took delivery of its first computer in 1961, "work study" and "organisation and method" teams were trained, modern accounting techniques were introduced, the first economist was appointed to the staff, and outside consultants were retained to examine some of the more specialised projects. In 1963 a Development and Steering Committee was set up, under the Chairmanship of the General Manager and including the heads of the commercial, operating, engineering, financial and economic departments. Forecasts at that time suggested that, given growth in the national economy at anything like the target of four per cent each year, a steady increase could be expected in the trade of the port.

The Rochdale Committee's view that development should be concentrated at Tilbury was a welcome confirmation of the P.L.A.'s intention. Tilbury was

Against a traditional background, the new-style container cranes came to Tilbury. The photograph shows the last containers being loaded on the *Jervis Bay* to open the Tilbury to Australia service in 1970.　　　　　　　　　　*Courtesy Overseas Containers Limited*

already an impressive group of docks, with four miles of quay and about twenty berths used by a score of shipping lines. Conventional ocean trade was mainly with West Africa, India, Pakistan, the Far East and Australia. There were two riverside terminals: the 1,000-feet cargo jetty completed in 1921 and the 1,142-feet passenger landing stage opened in 1930. In the main dock there was the No 1 berth which had been opened in 1957 as the Ocean Passenger Terminal, but where emphasis had moved to general cargo handling.

By the mid-'sixties the commitment to Tilbury for all major new development was complete. It had not been an easy decision to make. Mr Dudley Perkins, who became Director General of the P.L.A. in 1964, later recalled: "Tilbury had two obvious attractions. First, the P.L.A. owned a lot of undeveloped land there; secondly, road traffic to and from Tilbury could avoid the traffic congestion of London. However attractive these points seemed to anyone theorising in an office on Tower Hill on the boundary of the City of London, there was still one of those imponderable emotional objections to be considered. Very simply, it was that the great shipping lines who regarded London as their home port, or at least their European terminal port, would not welcome a home in distant Essex. It was said that they would fight to the death not to leave the Royal Docks, India and Millwall, or Surrey. Tilbury was too far from London—it was said. This is precisely where the element of speculation comes in. This element can be minimised by research and by employing outside consultants, as was done, but neither of them could state whether the choice of immediate capital development should be at Tilbury or elsewhere in the vast area that comprises the Port of London."

Encouraged by Rochdale to build more deep-water quays, the P.L.A. resolved to construct a new branch dock at Tilbury. A first phase of construction began in 1963, providing four berths, at which the first vessels were able to tie up in July 1966. Two of them incorporated in their design all that had been learnt in the upper docks about the best use of forklift trucks with palletised loads in high, open transit sheds; these were allocated to export traffic to India and Pakistan. Facing them, on the other side of the new dock, were two berths for RO/RO traffic, with special ramps so that vehicles could drive on and off vessels through bow and stern doors; a Transport Ferry Service to Antwerp kept these berths busy from their opening day. An existing berth elsewhere at Tilbury had earlier been adapted for a Swedish Lloyd U.K. Ltd ferry service to Gothenberg which carried containers as well as passengers and their cars. In its first year, that berth handled just under 300,000 tons of cargo, which the P.L.A. proudly proclaimed to be "probably a record for cargo passing over a berth in the port".

Well before the four berths of phase one of the new branch dock had been completed, the Authority obtained the Minister of Transport's approval of a second phase. Construction began in August 1965 of seven more deep-water

Packaged timber. Some of the most successful early experiments with unitised cargoes were made with forest products. Tilbury now provides four specialised berths for this traffic, which handle well over a million tonnes every year.   *Courtesy P.L.A.*

The standard container led to the development of the cellular container-ship. The photograph shows the O.C.L. vessel *Moreton Bay*.

Courtesy Overseas Containers Limited

berths. The P.L.A. was no longer an entirely free agent. In accordance with the Rochdale Committee's recommendation, the government brought into existence in July 1963 a National Ports Council, and a Harbours Act passed by Parliament in the following year gave this Council responsibility for preparing and supervising a national plan for port development. Any schemes costing more than £500,000 required the consent of the Minister, after he had consulted the N.P.C. The P.L.A., which was clear and bold in its thinking, managed to escape any lengthy process of discussion. It had already acquired a great deal of experience with "unitised" cargo. The basic idea was that goods should be packaged in such a way that they formed large units of regular shape and size. One method was to stack and secure small packages on wooden pallets. In the case of timber, several tons of boards of equal length (anything up to 24 feet) could be stacked in box shape and banded in metal. Experiments with packaged lumber began in the Surrey Commercial Docks in 1963 and within two years the increase in this form of handling had established a trend towards bigger bulk-carrier vessels, needing deeper water than was available in the Surrey Commercial basins or in the river outside. From March 1966, therefore, a berth was allocated for packaged lumber at Tilbury, where ships up to 30,000 dwt — three times the size of those which used the Surrey Commercial Docks — could be handled. By that time most softwood cargoes were arriving in London in packaged form and so the P.L.A. decided that three of the berths in the new Tilbury branch dock should be allocated to this traffic.

All seven of the berths in the second phase of the construction programme had been intended from the outset for unitised cargoes and there was confident talk of achieving throughputs of 500,000 tons a year on each berth, which was about four times better than the performance at a very efficient conventional cargo berth. The P.L.A. accepted an idea canvassed by the Rochdale Committee that, when possible, berths should be leased to companies as plain quay wall and apron, with an area of land behind, and that the lessee should provide the required equipment and buildings. Two contracts were quickly signed on this basis with companies handling packaged forest products. Plans for the other berths were kept flexible; the possibility of container berths was now much in mind. One of Dudley Perkins' first acts when he was appointed Director General was to check the latest American developments. Afterwards he related: "On February 10, 1964, in Port Elizabeth, New York, I watched the first container ship I had ever seen load and discharge some 8,000 tons of cargo in a day. The speed and efficiency convinced me that this was the pattern of future general cargo handling for the trans-ocean trade. By mid-1965 I was able to put to my Board a reasoned case for a completely new kind of dock development for London."

There remained many problems to be overcome. There was still no

A Rail Freightliner Terminal at Tilbury, seen above, operates on a 24-hour basis and moves containers rapidly to groupage depots in every part of Britain. *Courtesy P.L.A.*

international standard for container dimensions, and that inhibited the construction of handling equipment and of cellular ships. In 1965 the United Kingdom resolved to proceed unilaterally with a definition of standards. At about the same time the National Ports Council began an experiment designed to solve some of the problems inherent in the concept of through traffic from an inland container depot in one country to a similar depot in another. It was foreseen that the filling and discharging of containers — "stuffing" and "stripping", in the inelegant terms now used — would often be performed away from seaport areas. It was considered necessary, therefore, "to test clearance procedures and proper integration of the road, rail and sea segments of the total transportation".

Meanwhile the P.L.A. made its own investigations and assessments. Early in 1965, it commissioned consultants to make a detailed study of the pattern of U.K. trade on the ocean routes of the world, from source to destination, and of the proportion which was suitable for containerisation. Ten thousand firms were asked to provide information and the P.L.A.'s new computer analysed the material. The Martech Report, as it became known, established many facts which had previously been unknown and which were of great value to many others beside the P.L.A. A quarter of Britain's total export trade, it was shown, originated within thirty miles of London, and more than half within 105 miles. On the basis of this information, the P.L.A. decided that London, if it was to compete, would have to provide regular sailings to all parts of the world with a frequency matching that of Rotterdam and Antwerp; otherwise London would find itself merely providing a feeder service to these Continental ports. Calculations were made that a fully developed container berth, at 1965 prices, would cost about £2 millions and would take three years to construct, which was rather more than the time required to build a container ship. The port authority, therefore, needed to anticipate the decisions of the shipping lines and investment became an act of faith.

The new dock at Tilbury was taking shape while all the investigation and discussion proceeded. Early in 1966 the P.L.A Chairman, Lord Simon, visited America and again examined progress there. He reported back his conclusion that container services would be extended to the ocean trades "in the near future". A few months later Dudley Perkins confidently predicted that the Port of London was on the brink of a new era. "We have been thinking of the requirements for container operations for many years and our basic plans and indeed actual construction work are well in advance of specific commercial commitments," he said, adding the promise that the berths would be ready at Tilbury as soon as there were container ships to use them. The estimated date was early in 1968.

By the end of 1966, the P.L.A. commitment was absolute. Its annual report for that year stated: "The Authority are firmly convinced that there is a commercial need for a large and efficient trans-ocean container port in south-east England. In the absence of such facilities, British traders could become dependent on container shipping services operating through near-Continental ports . . . The Authority decided, therefore, to develop the new extension of Tilbury Docks to meet this need . . . The new Tilbury container facilities will provide Britain with its first major and fully integrated ocean container ship terminal, with seven container berths."

The Authority investigated every aspect of container operation. It calculated that the new-type berths would require twelve to twenty acres of open space behind them for the reception, marshalling, stacking and despatch of containers. If 10,000 to 15,000 tons of cargo were to be handled in the course of 24 hours, with containers loading and discharging simultaneously, sophisticated control systems would be necessary. Mechanised equipment needed careful consideration — for example, would ship-based or quay gantries be best? Discussions took place with the shipping lines. The flexible use of labour was a prime necessity; "I am certain that we must negotiate a sensible rate with dock-workers before the first container ship arrives," said Dudley Perkins. Finally, there were the complexities of charging; "the aim must be," said Perkins, "to quote one single charge from door to door, with one set of documents and one payment." The way had been prepared for that by a massive simplification of P.L.A. charging methods a few years earlier; in 1962 schedules of charges on imports had been reduced from 4,300 variants to about 100, and charges on exports from over 2,000 to a dozen.

Construction at Tilbury went forward swiftly throughout 1967 and by the end of that year most of the new berths had been completed. The new branch dock already had an appearance of continuous lively activity. As one entered it, the two berths on the right-hand side were busy with conventional cargo exports to India and Pakistan. Opposite them, nearer the river, the two RO/RO berths handled a steadily increasing number of Transport Ferry Service vehicles. Further up the dock, two packaged timber berths came into operation during the summer. Away to the left, by the river, work had commenced on the Bulk Grain Terminal, described in the previous chapter.

Before the end of 1967 the P.L.A. authorised work to commence on a third phase of the development. Tilbury had originally been built as a sea-rail terminal link, but the switch from rail to road haulage had been starkly evident there. Before the war only 12 per cent of cargoes discharged at Tilbury were removed by road vehicles; by 1959 seventy per cent left by road. Phase three, therefore, provided for a new perimeter road, a new main gate providing eight traffic lanes, three large vehicle parks, and a dual-carriageway link to main routes to the north and south. Additionally, however, a Rail Freightliner Terminal was to be provided, designed to handle 60,000 containers a year on two or three trains arriving and departing each day. Everything was to be ready by the end of 1968 for a spectacular debut by Tilbury as Britain's first full-scale ocean terminal for container ships.

Meanwhile, as individual new berths were completed, they were brought into service. In January 1968 the P.L.A. opened a common-user berth and European Unit Routes Ltd., a subsidiary of the P & O Group, used it for a regular container service to and from the Continent. Initially, using a small chartered vessel, it operated a service three times a week in each direction between Tilbury and Rotterdam. Within a couple of months a second vessel was required, so that there could be a daily sailing in each direction. After another month, there was an additional service to Dunkirk. By September much larger vessels had been introduced, and within two years the business had built up to five vessels carrying 1,000 containers on twelve sailings each week, linking Tilbury with Rotterdam, Antwerp and Dunkirk.

The success of this service indicated a danger which the P.L.A. had already discerned: that London might get only a feeder service from the Continental ports if it failed to match their facilities for ocean traffic. British and Continental ports were, by this time, engaged in fierce competition and hard bargaining. Liverpool and Southampton had container berths under construction, though on a smaller scale than at Tilbury. Both announced in the summer of 1968 that they had secured trans-Atlantic container services. Rotterdam and Antwerp had been as quick off the mark as London, with heavy investment in the middle 'sixties, with financial assistance from government or municipal sources. By the end of 1968 Antwerp and Rotterdam each claimed to be handling 1,250 containers a week.

Such was the background against which, in June 1968, the *American Lancer* berthed at Tilbury, discharged and loaded her containers, and sailed away on the following tide. It was the first "super-express" container service across the Atlantic, introduced immediately the United States Lines had taken delivery of their new vessels. Sailings were between a new container terminal at Port Elizabeth, Newark, and Tilbury, Rotterdam, and Hamburg. London, then, was in business as an ocean container terminal, neck-and-neck with any Continental rival and ahead of any other U.K. port. A superbly-equipped berth had been made ready on time, equipped with impressive new machinery: two 30-ton Paceco-Vickers Portainer cranes, each costing £20,000, and a fleet of Clark Van straddle-carriers — those strange crab-like legs-on-wheels which pick up containers and run them around or stack them two or three high. No less satisfactory, new flexible working arrangements essential for success had been negotiated with the trade unions. Traditional arrangements in gangs earning piece rates had given way to shed or area crews of up to twenty men on a regular weekly wage, available whenever a ship docked, even if it was overnight during a bank holiday week-end, and ready to tackle any of the jobs that needed to be done.

The stage was set for the next major achievement, which was to bring the Tilbury story to a climax. Three years earlier most of the major shipping companies in Britain had formed a consortium, Overseas Containers Ltd., which planned to switch most if not all the traffic between Europe and Australia to container ships. Nine new vessels were ordered, for delivery early in 1969, and Tilbury was chosen as the European terminal for the service. It was estimated that almost £500 millions a year of trade would be involved. The new service would provide door-to-door schedules of three weeks, which reduced previous passage times by a third. It was planned that the containers would be packed and unpacked at inland terminals, delivered to and from Tilbury by express trains and that ship turn-round times would be reduced from several weeks to no more than 24 hours. O.C.L. invested something like £80 millions in what was to be the most sophisticated operation of its kind anywhere in the world. To enable containers to be handled at the rate of almost one every minute, details of each one would be programmed into a computer, which would then decide the order in which they should be moved, stacked and despatched. Crane operators would be supplied information on video screens, and would have keyboard facilities to reply.

The new berth—No 39, just inside the new branch dock, running back almost to the riverside—was ready by February 1969 and agreement was reached with the appropriate trade union on wages and conditions for the P.L.A. dockers who would work there. The pattern was the same as that already accepted and working smoothly at No 40 berth opposite, where the United States Lines container service was handled.

As the new O.C.L. ships were about to come into service, there was a catastrophic development. Negotiations had been going on since the end of 1967 between the P.L.A. and independent port employers, on one side, and the trade unions on the other for a complete "new deal" covering wages and conditions of service. Most of the union members who would be directly affected still worked on traditional break-bulk cargo-handling operations; for those employed on the new container and unitised cargo berths special package deals had been negotiated. Now, early in 1969, a twelve-man committee of the Transport and General Workers Union decided to apply sanctions, to speed up a conclusion of the negotiations. They decreed that their members should refuse to operate any further new berths in accordance with the new-style package deals until such time as the wider negotiations had been completed.

This ban affected two services which were just about to begin: forest products traffic to the new Berth No 46, carried by Seaboard Pioneer Terminals Ltd., and the O.C.L. container service to and from Australia. At the last minute, O.C.L. switched its vessels to Antwerp; not until May 1970 was it able to berth one of them at Tilbury. Not only were the two new Tilbury berths out of operation during the period of sanctions; all progress with mechanisation of conventional berths in the upper docks was also stopped.

Lord Aldington, who by this time had taken over the chairmanship of the P.L.A., reported bleakly at the end of 1969: "The damage that this has done, not only to the year's results but to the reputation of the port, is incalculable." In fact, some calculations *could* be made, even then. Quite apart from its Australian service, O.C.L. had joined with German and Japanese shipping lines in an international consortium to operate giant container ships between Europe and the Far East, starting in 1971. The decision about a U.K. terminal for this service fell to be made in November 1969 — during the Tilbury trouble. Southampton made a bid for it, with a capacity of two million tons a year, and the agreement was signed. Southampton doubled its trade at a stroke; London lost the 800,000 tons of conventional traffic with the Far East which it had been handling each year, and ended one of its most historic trading links.

The Straddle Carrier is an entirely new piece of equipment for the container age. It lifts the largest containers and transports and stacks them as required.   *Courtesy P.L.A.*

CHAPTER EIGHT

The Human Factor

THE setback at Tilbury in 1969 was a sharp reminder that, in our present society, the policies and practices of organised labour can influence the development and performance of British industry quite as significantly as any decisions by management. The P.L.A., indeed, had recognised this fact. At an early point in the construction of the new container port, its chief executive had conferred with trade union representatives and had told them: "It is no use building magnificent docks and sheds and cranes unless our relationship with you, the men, is right. In terms of importance, I am now completely convinced that the relationship with the men who are going to work these facilities is the **most** important thing." How did it happen, then, that plans to establish a commanding lead by Tilbury as the principal U.K. container port were so dramatically frustrated?

The roots of every serious problem in the Port of London in recent years reach right back into history. The port has established great traditions; it has also generated bitter emotions and prejudices. Just as the traditions owe much to the foresight and dedication of many men who took pride in the work of the port, so the prejudices have sometimes been stimulated by men whose ambitions were not principally concerned with its well-being. The reality, however, is that human pride and ambition, greed and prejudice, have had only a marginal effect upon the course of events.

The dominant influence on port operation and port labour practices, until very recent times, was the irregularity in the flow of cargoes which arose from natural forces. In ancient times, the wool fleets sailed twice a year, at the seasons when the sheep were sheared. Later, as trade expanded, most of the main cargoes were seasonal: sugar from the West Indies, timber from the north, spices from the Far East. Furthermore, bad weather could hold back the arrival of a fleet by several weeks. The number of ships arriving weekly in London Dock in 1859 varied between 29 and 141. In a period of four successive weeks in 1861, West India Dock arrivals numbered 42, 131, 209 and 85. In the pre-machine age, when ship loading and discharge was a labour-intensive operation, the number of men required varied enormously from day to day, even from hour to hour, for there was very little advance notice that a ship was arriving.

Most labour in the port, therefore, was employed on a casual basis. Before the construction of the enclosed docks, there was a tight organisation of the men in the Watermen's Company, if they worked on the river, or in the various "brotherhoods" of porters licensed by the City Corporation. There was a general requirement that they should be Freemen of the City and the privileges were kept, so far as possible, in the same families by inheritance. Thus the available work was spread over a restricted number of men; though they were obliged to hold themselves ready to work when required between 4 a.m. and 8 p.m. in summer and between 6 a.m. and 6 p.m. in winter, each of them felt himself an independent craftsman. The "tackle porters" had a monopoly of all duties which required weights and scales, the "fellowship porters" handled all coal, corn, salt and other dry goods, the "ticket porters" had rights to work all American cargoes, and there were many other such specialised groups. This system had died out by the early part of the nineteenth century, as the new dock companies began to dominate the port.

The West India Dock Company, which was the first in business, seems to have started with high aspirations to create a permanent staff which would develop an *esprit de corps*. It recruited 200 permanent labourers and when

The Dockers' Call. The *Illustrated London News* published this artist's impression of the Call at the West India Docks in 1886.   *Mary Evans Picture Library*

there was no work for them on the quays, they were put to levelling and repairing roads. They were also obliged to join a Company regiment which was formed to protect the dock property. When the dock suddenly filled with ships, however, more labour was required. The Company established a system of "preference" men who were assured of a given number of days' work in the year. When this provision was inadequate, then other labourers were employed, on a casual basis, by the hour. The same system was adopted by other dock companies when they commenced operations. London Dock, in its early days, employed 300 permanent and preference labourers at a time when its average daily requirement was 1,000 to 1,200. St Katharine Dock opened in 1828 with 225 permanent and 200 preference men out of a maximum total employed of about 1,000.

Thus was established the system of twice-daily "calls" at each of the docks, when casual labour was hired for short periods. The men assembled on the pavements ready for work; those who were required were called, the others went home without reward. Some of the dock companies tried to give advance notice of the numbers which would be required, but with the uncertainties of sail, plus a surplus of labour, no such system was really workable. During the second half of the nineteenth century the indignity of men clamouring, and sometimes fighting one another, for the available jobs caused the dockland "calls" to become a symbol of the economic injustices of Victorian Britain. For a century and a half the casual nature of employment in the docks generated more bitterness and prepared the way more effectively for later industrial militancy than even low rates of pay.

When the docks first opened, wages and salaries were considered to be good, by the standards of the time. The West India Dock Company paid its permanent labourers 3s. 6d. a day; its top man, the dockmaster, received £630 a year, plus a bonus. When applying in 1823 for renewal of its monopoly, this Company pointed to "the marked improvement in the character of the labourers employed". The London Dock Company paid its foremen £100 a year, and required them to provide a security of £300, and its labouring coopers 18 shillings a week.

That the work was sought after on these terms is indicated by a minute of the Company in 1809 which decreed that vacancies for preference labourers should be filled by the directors in rotation, beginning with the chairman, the deputy chairman and the treasurer, and then by the others in alphabetical order. The hours of work were long: up to twelve hours in summer and ten hours in winter. Clerks turned up in frock-coats and labourers' dress included black waistcoats buttoned to the throat.

By the 1850s there was a serious degradation of conditions and pay. Henry Mayhew, the social commentator, visited every dock and many wharves and spoke to employers and labourers. He described in his *London Labour*

"The Dockers' Tanner" was the battle cry of the 1889 strike which began a tradition of militancy among London dockers. This photograph is of one of the street demonstrations.

and the London Poor how the frock-coats were worn through to the canvas and the waistcoats were ragged and greasy, how men were often without work for weeks and families lived by begging, how men worked the new cranes by treadmill and then went home to hovels. Years earlier, competition between the docks had led the companies to force down wages to fourpence an hour; an influx of labourers from Ireland, from the continent — and from the stricken English countryside — aided this process. Mayhew drew special attention to the inhumanity of the calls, when the casual labourers gathered to seek work. "Some men jump on the backs of others, so as to lift themselves high above the rest and attract the notice of him who hires them. All are shouting . . . It is a sight to sadden the most callous, to see thousands of men struggling for only one day's hire . . . For weeks many have gone there and gone through the same struggle, the same cries; and have gone away, after all, without the work they had screamed for." Mayhew contrasted this scene with the exotic cargoes on the quays: "There are acres upon acres of treasure, more than enough, one would fancy, to stay the cravings of the whole world." For those whose imaginations could not be stirred by words, the French artist Gustave Doré visited London and produced horrific illustrations of the dockland of the 1870s.

148

By this time, in the words of Marx, a spectre was haunting Europe. Whether it was a reverberating echo of the Paris Commune or whether it was born of fear as machines began to usurp some of the work of men, a deep spirit of unrest settled upon the Port of London.

The labourers' hourly rate was held down to fourpence for over forty years. Then trade unions came into existence to fight for more, and they developed their numbers and muscle in a series of strikes. An eight-day stoppage in the West India Dock in 1872 stirred up bitterness, but brought results to the men. The Company tried to recruit labour elsewhere, but failed; so it conceded an increase to fivepence an hour, and this was adopted throughout the port. Trade was buoyant at the time and the dock owners and wharfingers passed on their increased costs to their customers without difficulty. By the 'eighties, however, the situation had changed completely. The lightermen, the stevedores and the dockers were organised in unions, they had found an articulate leader in a young man called Ben Tillett, and they were in a mood to fight for more. They formulated their demands: a rise for labourers from fivepence to sixpence an hour, with eightpence an hour for overtime, and employment for periods of not less than half a day at a time. The dock companies were now in deep trouble. As we have seen in an earlier chapter, some were rushing towards insolvency and a patched-up emergency amalgamation which kept them afloat for a couple of decades until the Port of London Authority was set up. Faced then, in 1889, with a strike throughout the port, the employers refused even to discuss the men's demands and made it plain that they hoped to starve them back to work. Two early Labour leaders of great ability, John Burns and Tom Mann, assumed the leadership of the strikers and focused popular attention on their case. Day after day dockers' processions marched from East London to Hyde Park, carrying not only the union banners but also bits of fish, meat and vegetable stuck on poles, to show what the dockers' meagre diet was like. Popular sympathy was roused not only in Britain, but also to a remarkable degree in Australia. Brisbane waterfront labourers launched a fund which, in a short time, raised £30,000 from a wide section of the Australian public. The strike organisation, which had been on the brink of collapse, was reinforced, and there was talk of a general strike in London and a body of public men led by the Lord Mayor of London and the Roman Catholic Archbishop, Cardinal Manning, then put pressure on the dock companies' directors. Terms were negotiated which gave the dockers most of what they wanted, including a basic sixpence an hour and a minimum engagement of four hours. With this victory, trade unionism was firmly established throughout the port and was given a fillip throughout the nation. To this day, the "Great Strike of 1889 which won the Dockers' Tanner" is a shining chapter in the history of the organisation of British labour. Perhaps more important, there are men in the docks today whose great-grandfathers played their part in that struggle, and some part of the emotions generated have been transmitted through the generations.

After 1889 there was no serious industrial trouble in the port until 1911, apart from a three months strike of lightermen in 1900. But social conditions in the East End had become appalling and political reformers argued with passion, and with good reason, the need for a transformation of society. Beyond the Sailors' Town, just east of the Tower of London, where the shops were full of nautical clothing, instruments and stores, there lay Wapping, Shadwell and Limehouse, the poorest and shabbiest district of London, where destitution and drunkenness had brought life down to a brutish level. We have it on the authority of respected Labour historians G. D. H. Cole and Raymond Postgate that "when John Burns spoke on Tower Hill to his dockers, only a small part of his speeches was devoted to union demands; a large section was turned to urging them to behave as human beings—not to beat their wives, not to fight one another savagely, not to drink themselves stupid at the first opportunity . . .".

Against this general background, it is not surprising that, in the words of one of the employers, "labour became difficult to handle" in the years after the great strike. Beset by their own serious financial problems, the employers' morale was low. In this situation, they made one decision which added greatly to difficulties in the docks, creating new problems which had not been solved nearly ninety years later.

When the West India Dock first opened, none but the Company's own labourers were permitted to handle cargoes, and this policy was followed elsewhere; but not everywhere, the London Dock Company, for example, offering shipowners the option of using their own ships' crews or of employing their own labourers. Over the years, however, the dock companies, as well as providing the quays, sheds, cranes and other facilities, had employed the labour. After 1889 the shipowners sought to reclaim and extend their theoretical right to employ labour for loading and discharge of cargoes, arguing that they might then avoid the delays which had resulted from strikes and stoppages. The Chairman of the London and India Joint Committee which had taken charge of the port, Mr C. M. Norwood, thought it might relieve the dock companies of a large part of their problems if the shipowners' claim was conceded. He was opposed initially by every other member of the Committee, but he had his way. It was eventually agreed that at the Victoria, the Albert and the Tilbury Docks shipowners should be free, if they wished, to employ their own labour to handle goods, on the quays as well as on board ship. Sheds and cranes would be made available to them on hire, under a "quay and shed space agreement". These new rules meant that every shipowner could be a law unto himself as regards conditions and terms of labour. Where, in the Royal Docks, there had been a single employer, there

Ben Tillett, the sailor who came ashore, formed a union and led the first great dock strike in 1889. *T.U.C. Library*

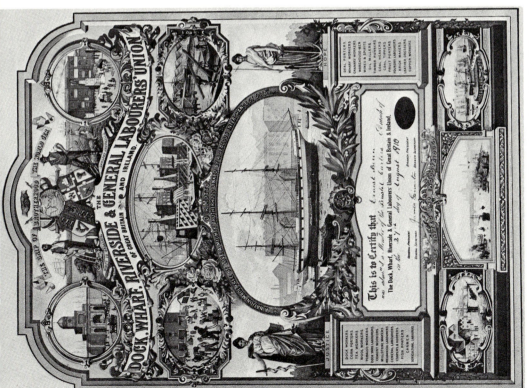

This membership certificate of one of the early unions in the Port of London, the Dock, Wharf, Riverside and General Labourers' Union, shows that despite the hardships there was pride in the port and its activities. This is the certificate issued to a new recruit, Ernest Bevin, on 27th August, 1910

Courtesy Transport & General Workers' Union

were now a score. Firms of master stevedores came into existence to take over the responsibilities which had been those of the dock companies' superintendents. The number of call-on points for casual labour increased.

The Joint Committee took another decision which set a pattern for years ahead. It decided to employ itself four different classes of labour: a permanent staff entitled to holidays and sick pay and pensions; registered, or "A", labourers employed on a weekly basis; preference, or "B", labourers, who were given tickets numbered according to their seniority and who had first call on available work after the "A"s; and, finally, the casuals.

In 1911, two years after the establishment of the P.L.A., the various trade unions in the port came together to form the National Transport Workers' Federation and almost immediately it approached the P.L.A. for a wage increase to eightpence an hour, improved conditions, and formal recognition of all the unions. Lord Devonport, the Chairman of the P.L.A., called a conference of port employers, with wharfingers and shipowners represented, and this produced what was termed "The Devonport Agreement", which offered the dockers sevenpence an hour and a one-hour reduction in the working day. The cost to the employers was £200,000 a year, but the unions, who had secured no improvements since 1889, felt they were being rushed into acceptance of too little, too late. At first there seemed a chance that they would accept the offer, but after a meeting of the dockers it was rejected, and Devonport behaved like a man betrayed. He refused further negotiations and publicly declared that he would see the men starved into submission. Ben Tillett led a mass meeting of dockers on Tower Hill in a prayer: "Oh God, strike Lord Devonport dead." After a strike lasting a fortnight, the men went back to work on Devonport's terms.

A notable feature of that strike was that it represented a first effort to impose a closed shop in the docks. One of the union conditions, which was met initially, but later withdrawn, was that men recruited by the shipowners should be engaged *outside* the dock gates, which would have enabled union membership to be checked before the men were able to offer themselves for work. The closed shop issue arose again in 1912, when lightermen refused to work with a man alleged to have broken union rules. The whole of the port stopped work, but midway through the strike the union switched its main demand to increased pay and shorter hours. The employers refused to meet or to talk and after ten weeks the union leaders ordered the men back.

A clash of will occurred during this period which, unremarked at the time, may have had profound effects upon the course of events in the docks industry in later years. A young union organiser in Bristol called Ernest Bevin addressed an appeal to Devonport, as the employers' principal spokesman, urging a spirit of conciliation. Devonport, whose authoritarian streak was strongly evident at the time, ignored the letter, considering it an impertinence.

152

Bevin went on to maintain a life-long campaign on behalf of the dockers and, arguably, to have a more profound effect upon the port industry than any other single individual at any time.

The First World War diverted energies from industrial strife and brought a steady increase in port workers' earnings. When it was over the unions moved to consolidate their gains and advance further, and in 1920 a Court of Inquiry was set up to consider their wages, their conditions, and the casual nature of their employment. At the twenty public sessions of the Court the dockers' spokesman was Ernest Bevin, and his advocacy won him the popular title of "The Dockers' K.C." and a national reputation. It led, also, to a new minimum wage of sixteen shillings a day, a 44-hour week and the first system of registration of dock labour.

The unions had sought to control registration themselves, but the Committee rejected this idea. A joint Registration Committee, with seven employers' and seven union representatives, was created. It listed 37,118 recognised port workers in London and issued each of them with a numbered brass disc, or "tally". No-one without a tally could work in the port. The number of men registered was gradually reduced over the years and recruitment was closed to outsiders; when a limited number of new men were taken on, preference was given to the sons of dockers. The brass tallies remained in use until 1927, when they were replaced by registration books, to which were attached the holders' unemployment insurance books. All this was but a tiny step towards the form of port industry organisation of which Ernest Bevin dreamt.

In 1931 he and Ben Tillett were among the members of yet another Committee of Inquiry and there they fought for "a minimum weekly income, pensions, registration *and distribution of employment under one statutory authority.*" The cost could be met, they argued, by a levy on all goods and passengers through the ports. They did not persuade the Committee, and again Bevin had to bide his time.

Meanwhile, during those years between the two world wars, unions and employers fell back into the postures of confrontation. In 1922 Bevin created the Transport and General Workers' Union. It did not immediately strengthen overall union organisation, for many stevedores and lightermen refused to join it and created a new organisation of their own, the National Amalgamated Stevedores, Lightermen, Watermen, and Dockers Union. In 1927 this union split into two parts: the National Amalgamated Stevedores and Dockers Union and the Watermen, Lightermen, Tugmen and Bargemen's Union. Inter-union competition frequently added to the problems of men and managements.

During a slump in 1923 the employers proposed a reduction in wages from eight shillings to 5s. 6d. for the half-day minimum employment period. The dockers struck work, but after being out for eight weeks went back beaten

Ernest Bevin, the young union leader, at the time he made his reputation as "The Dockers' K.C." Later he became a powerful Cabinet Minister and was influential in securing a transformation of labour relations in the ports. *T.U.C. Library*

and sullen. Eight months passed and then Bevin slapped in a demand for seven shillings for the half-day. The employers offered six shillings. Bevin went to see Devonport at the P.L.A., who told him curtly: "Our offer is one shilling — do what you will." He may have said more, for Bevin later told a Court of Inquiry that he would never again negotiate with Devonport unless he apologised for a comment which Bevin called "the greatest insult ever offered by an employer to a trade union leader". Bevin called another strike, it was a short sharp struggle, and the union won.

Emotions had certainly not settled by the time the British General Strike of 1926 occurred. What had been seen as a union-bosses conflict then took on the aspect of open class war, indeed, some thought, of revolution; and some of the most dramatic episodes were played out in the Port of London. Vast quantities of perishable food stores lay in its warehouses and, when the strikers announced that power supplies would be cut, the government resolved to move these cargoes. Anti-strike volunteers, with naval assistance, loaded the goods inside the docks, and hundreds of lorries driven by soldiers of crack Guards regiments carried them away. A destroyer anchored in the river close to the Royal Docks, and another near the Surrey Commercial group. Armoured cars manned by men of the Royal Tank Corps convoyed the lorries as they left the docks amid the angry shouts of dockers and their families. And, at some points near dock gates, the dockers stared at machine-guns which they believed were directly aimed at them.

This trauma passed, but it left an inheritance of bitterness which infected the port for generations afterwards and made difficult a solution of any of the very real problems which developed. By the early 'thirties over a third of

154

Britain's port workers were drawing unemployment pay and, at the same time, there were the first, tentative moves to mechanise some port operations. The appearance of a 150-tons self-propelled floating crane, the *London Mammoth*, aroused a wave of indignation and suspicion. Only the outbreak of another war set the port on a new and more positive course.

When Winston Churchill formed his coalition government in 1940 he understood that the trades unions had developed such power that their full co-operation was essential to successful mobilisation of man-power for the war effort. He understood, too, that there was one man who was uniquely qualified to deliver full union commitment and to call forth an unqualified response from ordinary men and women. That man was Ernest Bevin, whose career had been launched with his performance as "The Docker's K.C." and was now to go forward as one of the most powerful ministers in Britain's War Cabinet. As Minister of Labour he produced in 1941 a regulation which became known as "The Dockers' Charter", bringing into existence the following year a National Dock Labour Corporation, which was to register and pay a basic weekly wage to all dock workers who were not on the regular staff of a port employer. The system was perpetuated, when the war was over, by a Dock Workers (Regulation of Employment) Order which came into effect on 1st July, 1947. A National Dock Labour Board became the employer of all registered port workers and individual employers (of whom there were more than 300 in London) drew from this pool the men for whom they had work. The employers paid the wages, plus a percentage levy, to the Dock Labour Board, which paid the men. The call system continued, so that the casual nature of employment was still not removed, but men were paid "attendance money" — a guaranteed weekly wage of £4 8s. whether or not there was work to be done — and holiday pay. London had its own local Dock Labour Board, under the aegis of the national organisation. Membership was drawn equally from employers and unions, each side providing a joint chairman. Decasualisation had still to be achieved, but the role of the port employer had been curbed; not only terms and conditions of employment, but disciplinary procedures in the industry, had to be fully agreed with the unions.

Ironically, as the unions established their new rights, they showed signs of losing the support of their members. Unofficial leaders emerged in the various docks, co-ordinated their efforts through a Liaison Committee, and led a series of major strikes which often had no direct relevance to dockers' pay or conditions. The Transport and General Workers' Union was particularly criticised for being out of touch with its members. Others attributed the trouble to the activities of a handful of politically inspired extremists. A particular example of the disruption caused in the port was a strike in the summer of 1949, which followed the refusal of some dockers to discharge two Canadian ships because their crews were on strike. The government declared a state of emergency and troops moved into the dock to handle cargoes. The Transport and General Workers' Union expelled three of its members who had led the strikers. As a protest against these expulsions, another strike was called, and again the troops moved in. And so it went on. In 1951 the Attorney General instigated proceedings against seven of the unofficial militant dockers' leaders, and again there were strikes. In 1957 there was an unofficial strike to show solidarity with porters working in London's big fruit and vegetable market in Covent Garden and the following year a similar one in support of porters and drivers in the Smithfield meat market. Dockers' wages went up year by year and the working week was reduced, but the militancy remained. In 1961 the government set up yet another committee to probe every aspect of ports operation.

The Rochdale Committee, taking its name from its Chairman, Viscount Rochdale, made sweeping proposals for reorganisation of the ports industry, and an important part of its report dealt with labour relations. It recommended that decasualisation should be taken to the point where the twice daily call for men should be discontinued. It declared that there were too many employers, particularly in the Port of London, to make it practicable for men to be employed on a regular basis, and that only "substantial firms" with a steady and continuing demand for labour could establish satisfactory working relationships. It proposed, therefore, that small firms should be encouraged to amalgamate and that only approved firms which could meet certain minimum qualifications should be admitted to the National Dock Labour Board registers. If this was achieved, greater mobility of labour would become possible, maximum use of mechanical aids, and a reduction in the number of dockers. "Fear of redundancy is very real among dock workers, as is their concern that the benefits of mechanisation should be fairly shared," the Committee reported. "With goodwill and mutual trust between the parties there should be no insuperable difficulty in determining fair and realistic manning scales."

Many recommendations of the Rochdale Committee were acted upon by the Conservative government of the day, but those affecting dock workers remained on the table until, in the autumn of 1964, a new Labour ministry came to office. Labour had written into its programme a commitment to nationalise the ports industry, and one of its first acts in government was to set up a further committee, headed by Lord Devlin, to consider the treatment of dock labour. The Devlin Report, and its acceptance by the government, marked the end, at last, of the system of casual employment which had been the gushing fount of dockland grievance since times beyond memory. Devlin developed the Rochdale proposals. The call system must end. Port workers must be employed on a regular basis. Only employers who could constantly employ sufficient men to form an economic unit should be licensed to remain in business. On the basis of this new deal, restrictive practices operated by labour should be eliminated.

Parliament passed the Docks and Harbours Act to implement these proposals and a Dock Modernisation Committee was set up to supervise the reforms. In London the P.L.A. became the licensing authority for employers; it issued licences to 208 private firms and it allocated the number of permanent men each employer, including itself, should take at the commencement of the new system. Among the firms registered were 130 wharfingers, 49 lightermen and tug operators, 13 cargo superintending companies, ten general stevedoring companies operating in the enclosed docks and six others operating elsewhere. Forty-seven would-be employers were refused registration.

The National Dock Labour Scheme, with its London Board composed half of employers and half of union nominees, remained unchanged and regulated recruitment, dismissal, discipline, welfare and training matters. Whereas the register it maintained had previously guaranteed priority to men in seeking work, in the new circumstances it guaranteed men permanent jobs from which they could only be sacked if found guilty of theft or assault while on port property. Moreover, employers could no longer engage particular individuals they might have preferred; they stated their need and received an allocation from the register.

The pendulum had certainly swung to the opposite quarter. The P.L.A. and the independent employers found their costs substantially increased under this new system. The lighterage industry reported an increase of 16 per cent.

Deal porters in the Surrey Docks formed one of the groups with specialised skills of which they were fiercely proud, though the work was hard and dangerous.
P.L.A. Collection, Museum of London

157

The P.L.A. expressed its hope that the additional costs would be recouped "when the rest of the reorganisation recommended by the Devlin Committee was achieved and all the age-long practices which had grown up to protect labour from the worst effects of casual employment were abandoned". Negotiations on these matters—described as Devlin Phase Two—were scheduled to follow hard on the heels of decasualisation.

It was now 1967, the future pattern of port operation in the age of containers and bulk and unitised cargoes had clearly emerged, and the need to end the age-old restrictive practices had become urgent for management. For a century and more, while the dice had been so heavily loaded against the port labourer, great ingenuity and determination had gone into devising a wide variety of restrictions which had the practical effect of spreading the available work as widely as possible. Men had worked in gangs, often the same men together on a regular basis, and a system of manning levels and piecework rates for particular cargoes and conditions had been evolved. The rates which could be earned varied considerably according to circumstances. To prevent "blue-eyed boys" favoured by foremen getting all the lucrative work, a so-called "continuity rule" was applied, obliging a worker to complete a particular job once he had started it, and there was reluctance to work overtime. This meant that gangs could not take the highest-earning part of a job and then move on to something else, and they could not work overtime to complete a job. As a corollary, jobs could not be started in the middle of a turn. By narrowing down the definition of a job to one particular hatch of a ship, maximum benefit was secured for the maximum number of men. It should be added that in some circumstances the continuity rule worked to the employers' advantage, too.

Over the years, bargaining about piece rates had created a tangle of figures, many of them the result of *ad hoc* arrangements to meet particular emergencies and never formalised in the piece rate book. In 1970 Lord Pearson, presiding over yet another Committee of Inquiry, concluded: "The existing wage arrangements are so complex, irrational and varied that the task of sorting them out . . . would certainly be long and difficult and probably impossible."

Thus it was urgent that Devlin Phase Two negotiations should produce new conditions of service to suit the new conditions. In particular, the P.L.A. called for the abolition of piece work, more flexible manning of quays and ships, and the introduction of shift working. The Transport and General Workers' Union favoured these changes, at the right price. The rival National Amalgamated Stevedores and Dockers' Union opposed shift working. Some of the independent port employers were unhappy about the abolition of piece work, fearing a fall in productivity. Perhaps not surprisingly, the negotiations went forward very slowly. As they dragged on, the P.L.A. negotiated special "package deals" with the union to cover individual Tilbury berths as they were completed. In this situation, when the talking had been going on for well over a year and no agreement was in sight, the Transport and General Workers' Union committee concerned with south-eastern ports imposed the ban which prevented O.C.L. opening their new container service to Australia on schedule.

In September 1970 the Phase Two agreement was at last signed. Port workers secured basic weekly wages well in advance of anything they had had previously; piece work was abolished; a two-shift system within a 31¼ hours week was introduced on the new berths; the whole labour scene changed to a more flexible use of men and machines.

All who had been involved in the negotiations and all who were concerned with creating a new and more prosperous future for the Port of London had come to appreciate, in the words of Lord Rochdale, that "few industries are so burdened with the legacy of the past". Now, perhaps the score had been settled. The dream of Ernest Bevin had been realised, the unions' long campaign had been won.

But in the hour of triumph, the prize crumbled in the dockers' hands.

Lightermen working on the river navigated their dumb craft with 30-feet "sweeps" and could "drive" for twelve miles on a tide. They were Members of the Company of Watermen and as conscious of the great traditions of their calling as of the daily hazards they faced.

P.L.A. Collection, Museum of London

CHAPTER NINE

Ebb and Flow

THE acceptance of the Devlin Committee's recommendations by the Labour government of the day marked the beginning of what should have been a new era of hope in the port, but what proved to be one of the most difficult and often depressing periods in its twentieth-century history. For employers and workers there seemed to be promise of a new deal and a more prosperous future, but the promise did not survive for more than a few months. The unions had at last buried the hated system of casual employment; every dock worker was now to receive regular wages. The employers, because freight liners had begun to operate to regular timetables and radio and telex provided advance information to permit detailed planning, could assess their labour requirements more accurately than ever before and could spread the work more evenly in time. For the first time, there were no inherent problems in the policy of decasualisation — the industry had evolved to the point at which a permanent labour force was appropriate to its needs. This was true, however, only if the number of men employed on the new permanent basis accurately matched the continuous flow of cargoes. In fact, the 23,000 men registered in the port were far more than were required; during the early months of 1967, three thousand were idle each day. In no circumstances, however, could men be made redundant or compulsorily retired.

It had been foreseen that the switch to containers would reduce the number of jobs, but hardly anyone understood the speed at which events would move. The Minister of Labour, for example, expressed confidence in 1967 that the natural eight per cent per year "wastage" of manpower from the industry, plus a reduction in the retirement age from sixty-eight to sixty-five, would keep men and jobs in reasonable balance. A "voluntary severance" scheme was introduced, offering cash sums of from £200 to £600 to the older men if they left, and in London the great majority accepted this offer. But the problem of surplus labour grew monstrously.

Devlin offered regular employment to those who worked in the port. The National Dock Labour Scheme, which was perpetuated in the new circumstances, *guaranteed every registered man* a weekly wage . . . even although it soon became clear that there was not sufficient work available in the port to occupy the men. The unions were adamant, and were backed by the government, that redundancy could be dealt with only by "voluntary severance" with cash compensation; those who did not choose to take this option would, if there was no work for them, fall back on the guaranteed weekly minimum wage.

The financial burden which was thus imposed on the industry might have been successfully carried if the second phase of Devlin, bringing more flexibility and efficient use of manpower, had been quickly implemented. In fact, the negotiations between port employers and trade unions went on for two and a half years. During that time productivity in the port declined seriously, charges were raised, and trade was lost.

Within seven weeks of the signing of the Phase II agreement in September 1970, the P.L.A. announced that throughput in the enclosed docks had declined by 23 per cent, and in this period 90 ships were diverted from London. The general view was that these were teething troubles and that all would come right. Certainly, the dockers could not be given all the blame. An employers' spokesman declared in January 1971 that less than four hours of productive work was being performed in the new 6¼ hours shifts in the enclosed docks. He estimated a loss of 65 minutes per man per shift because of late starts, early finishes and extended meal-times; the unions retorted, fairly enough, that bad time-keeping was as much to do with management as with workers. In any case, 80 minutes per shift was being lost because of difficulties with road transport and lighterage, equipment delays, or bad weather.

The results were catastrophic. By March 1971 there was a crisis, tonnages handled of conventional cargo were 25 to 30 per cent below pre-Devlin II

Viscount Simon, Chairman of the Port of London Authority, 1958-71.   *Courtesy P.L.A.*

levels, and traffic was departing. By the summer the average number of ships in the port at any one time was about 50, compared with 80 a year earlier. On top of this, there then came a serious down-turn in world trade, and the labour surplus in the port was then the biggest problem. The higher basic wage resulting from Devlin had to be paid when traffic was being turned away because of reduced productivity, and it had to be paid when the traffic had largely disappeared and there was insufficient work to go round. Either way, the port suffered.

By 1975 it was generally accepted that incentives had to be restored. A bonus paid on an area-shift basis, to a large group of men, was first tried and after six months productivity was reported up 27 per cent and ship turn-round times down by 28 per cent. In 1978 this "primary bonus" was supplemented by a smaller bonus paid on a ship-gang or unit basis, and again productivity was reported up, by 20 per cent in the first two months.

Long before the Devlin Phase II agreement had raised this productivity problem, a considerable number of private employers in the Port of London were in financial difficulties, and many went out of business. As they did so, they returned their dock labour to the central pool, from which it was re-allocated to those firms which survived, accentuating *their* problems. At the same time, the P.L.A. closed down two of its principal dock systems, and a number of berths elsewhere. The surplus of dock workers threatened to reach catastrophic proportions.

The idea of "severance" payments to men who left the industry voluntarily, was, therefore, established on a more or less permanent basis. The London port employers produced a scheme in 1968 which offered "severance" to every man in the port, whatever his age; the cash offered was related to the number of years of service and those who had been working in the port for over twenty-five years were able to collect £1,800 to £2,000. Unfortunately, the implementation of this scheme was delayed by arguments about its organisation and financing. The government had committed itself to nationalisation of the port industry; the employers, consequently, wanted to know whether the large sums they were proposing to pay out would be taken into the reckoning when compensation was paid at the time of a state take-over. In the end, no nationalisation took place, for the Labour government was defeated at the polls in 1969 and the next Labour administration, during the 'seventies, paid lip-service to the principle but did not introduce a bill into Parliament.

Eventually the severance scheme got going, the government made a loan of £3½ millions, and the understanding was reached that the cost would be collected from the port employers over a period of time in the form of a levy related to their aggregate wage bills. By August 1969 a total of 1,108 men — 827 dockers and 281 lightermen — had taken severance and there was a disposition in some quarters to believe that the necessary reduction had been

Dudley Perkins, P.L.A. Director-General 1964-71, the period which saw the impact of the container revolution.
Courtesy P.L.A.

achieved. By the end of that year, however, London employers were forecasting a surplus of 1,500 men in the first part of 1970. And so it continued, year after year, the rate of severance payments increasing steadily, to maxima of £5,000 in 1975 and £7,000 in 1977 for the longest-serving men. The number on the register went down dramatically: from 23,000 in 1967 to 16,500 in 1971 and to only 8,800 by 1977. But yet, at any time during the years, there were always far too many men for the work to be done, and it remained so even in 1978.

A particular aspect of the problem was the disproportionate number of aged and medically unfit men. There had been no regular recruitment of young dock workers for a generation. The introduction of shift working from 1970 emphasised how serious this imbalance had become. Later, in 1975, when one of the largest private firms in the port found itself in difficulties and was taken over by the P.L.A., it was found that 500 of its 2,670 registered dock workers were in the medically restricted category. At one point in the summer of 1977 eleven per cent of the men working in the P.L.A. enclosed docks were away sick.

Alongside the surpluses of men in some locations, there were actual shortages at the new berths at Tilbury. Payments of £1,050 were then made to

163

some men in the Upper Docks to encourage them to transfer permanently to Tilbury, and there was also some limited recruitment to the industry.

Employment and severance policies have been determined by the National Dock Labour Board in accordance with government thinking and membership of the Dock Labour Boards is evenly balanced between employers and unions. This provided an assurance that the human problems which inevitably arise when a great industry is rapidly contracting were handled sympathetically. Mr Jack Jones, the then General Secretary of the Transport and General Workers' Union, wrote with evident pride and satisfaction in 1977: "In the case of the docks industry not one man has been compulsorily dismissed due to redundancy and in no other industry have manual workers been offered the high level of voluntary severance payments. There has been a greater move to shorter working hours, too, in the ports, particularly in the enclosed docks of London, than in any other section of industry and again the guaranteed payments whether men are working or not are much higher in the docks industry."

The trade unions had found they had the muscle to compel these favourable terms. From the employers' side, there were warnings that the short-term benefits were being taken at the risk of long-term disaster. Lord Aldington repeatedly cautioned during the two years leading up to his retirement from the chairmanship of the P.L.A. in 1977 that the industry could not afford the cost of surplus manpower. At some periods during 1976, he said, the Authority had been paying £150,000 a week to men for whom there was no work. "There is no reason at all why the P.L.A. should not be profitable so long as the conditions under which it employs dock workers and staff are reasonable and sensible, and competition is fair," he wrote. "Ways have to be found of reducing the cost to the employers of men for whom there is no work. I regard the release of surplus people, both registered dock workers and others, as essential to the survival of the P.L.A. as an autonomous trust port."

Under a new Chairman, Sir John Cuckney, the nettle was grasped. But by then the Port of London Authority was virtually insolvent and the struggle ahead, back to efficient and viable port operation, looked a long, hard one.

The big contraction in the port took place in the late 'sixties and early 'seventies. Much of St Katharine Dock, badly bombed during the war, was never restored, though the old Dock House was redeveloped as an office block. By the time the Devlin Committee reported, the P.L.A. had sold off the old East India Dock and had decided that London Dock, which was being run at a loss, must also close. It discharged its last ship in September 1968. By that time parts of the Surrey Commercial complex on the other side of the river were being filled in, beginning with the Lady Dock and part of Lavender Dock. In the summer of 1969 the decision was made to close the whole Surrey Commercial group and on 22nd December, 1970, the Russian timber vessel

Kandalakshales was the last ship to sail from an enclosed dock on the south side of the Thames.

During the summer of 1969 the P.L.A. made a completely fresh assessment of its future needs and prospects and amended the five-year programme it had prepared in 1967. The revised plan involved closing within five years half of the 108 conventional general cargo berths still being used in the remaining enclosed docks. The Director-General called together 350 delegates representing the port workers and he described to them the prospect for the 'seventies. Trade would expand, he thought, particularly container, oil and bulk cargo traffic, but conventional cargo would decline and there would be a steady reduction in the labour required. He pointed out that some countries were insufficiently industrialised to enable them to get full benefit from containerisation; to serve their needs the Millwall Dock would be developed to handle palletised cargoes. The aim was to create "a compact group of modern mechanised berths sufficient to handle the traffic offered".

This was a difficult period for the nation as a whole. The level of trade had declined, the government had imposed restrictions on imports to protect the balance of payments, sterling had been devalued in 1967, and inflation was beginning to emerge as a serious problem. With the relentless pressure to

No. 19 shed in the South West India Dock was completed in 1967 (then known as "M" Shed) and it set new standards. There was direct road access to ground and first floors, each providing 81,500 square feet of space. Another floor was used for warehousing. *Courtesy P.L.A.*

reduce the number of port jobs, a fear of unemployment emerged and a general feeling of uncertainty undermined morale. A number of industrial disputes occurred. In 1970 there was the first *official* strike in the port for forty-four years, and in 1972 there was a three-weeks national dock strike.

The P.L.A. was not the only port organisation under serious strain. Many of the wharfingers and lighterage firms operating on the Thames were unable or unwilling to carry the additional costs imposed by decasualisation. Between September 1967 and January 1970 thirty-two riverside wharves closed down. One after the other all the historic wharves around the Pool and along the Wapping water-front put up their shutters and fell silent. Sea-going ships were no longer seen from Tower Bridge and by the early 'seventies there was not a single job for a docker along half a mile of riverside where 5,000 had been working only five years earlier.

Lighterage had been in decline for many years already: the number of lightermen at work on the river fell from 5,000 in 1959 to 2,000 in 1969. From the autumn of 1967 the pace of this decline greatly increased. In little over two years sixteen lighterage firms collapsed and by 1971 the independent Waterman, Lightermen, Tugmen and Bargemen's Union was so depleted that it was absorbed by the T. and G.W.U. By the end of 1976 there were only 887 registered lightermen left.

One of the most traumatic closures was that of Hays Wharf in 1969. The company concerned owned a long stretch of famous Tooley Street wharves which for three-hundred years had been regarded as "the larder of London" because of their trade in butter, cheese, bacon and other provisions. In May the management announced the closure of their Mark Brown wharf, which employed 276 men. They declared that in the period since decasualisation there had been 123 minor stoppages of work by gangs working on this wharf, that this was very serious when perishable cargoes were being handled, and that they had lost a contract for trade with Poland which was the wharf's main activity. The unions reacted strongly and the London Dock Labour Board refused to let the Hays Wharf company return all 276 men to the labour pool. The Board agreed to accept 179, but then asked Hays Wharf to take back 49 of these as its share of the "reallocated labour force". The management thereupon firmly protested, insisting that its number of workers must be drastically reduced. Criticism and counter-criticism rumbled on until, before the end of the year, the Hays Wharf company pulled out entirely from its riverside activity and all the wharves were closed.

Later the management asserted that a combination of RO/RO containers and modern marketing methods had put them out of business: their warehouses were superfluous when provisions were containerised through Tilbury direct to the inland stores set up by supermarket chains. The dockers refused to accept the management explanations and argued that some riverside activities were being moved elsewhere so that there would be no obligation to employ registered dock labour. Thus opened a new phase of struggle. The T. and G.W.U. announced that it had reported at least twenty firms to the London Dock Labour Board because they were employing non-registered men to do what was claimed as port work. There were, indeed, new container depots away from the immediate port area in which non-registered men were working. The unions referred to these contemptuously as "one man and a dog operations" and "lump-type labour without agreed manning scales". Because of the way in which dockers' jobs were disappearing week by week, much emotion was generated by this new issue. Militant dockers picketed some of the new depots, one of the employers took proceedings in the National Industrial Relations Court, five of the pickets went to prison, and a new strike flared.

The Labour government, which was still in power at that time, appointed the Bristow Committee to consider how more accurately to define what was rightly "dock work" and what was meant by "the vicinity of the port". The proposal which emerged was for a five miles corridor on each side of the river, within which all container depots must employ registered dock labour. As with the proposed nationalisation plan, a change of government ruled out any such action, at least until Labour returned to power in 1974. Even then, Parliament did not receive the proposal sympathetically and as late as 1978 it was unclear whether the corridor scheme would ever be applied.

Though it disliked the Bristow formula, the Conservative government of 1969-74 could not duck the main issue. In 1972 one of the larger independent companies, Southern Stevedores, went out of business and its 1,200 workers were returned to the pool of labour. The government set up a new committee, jointly led by Lord Aldington, the chairman of the P.L.A., and Mr Jack Jones, the General Secretary of the T. and G.W.U., to assess the real labour requirements of the port and to devise means of creating more jobs for unemployed dockers. The two men rushed out a report within a matter of weeks. They urged the port authorities, other employers and the unions to make greater efforts to create new jobs, particularly by opening more container depots for "groupage" work: the filling and emptying of containers with goods from or to a number of different customers. In the Port of London 173 additional jobs were quickly created. The P.L.A. took over existing groupage operations in the docks, established the Comprehensive Shipping Group, in which it took a 75 per cent interest, and opened the Comclear Terminal on the south side of the Royal Victoria Dock to develop international freight forwarding business.

A more important Aldington-Jones recommendation, however, was that the "temporarily unemployed register", which was composed of the men for whom there was no work but who were drawing the £23 guaranteed minimum weekly wage, should be abolished. This meant that every man on the register

Riverside wharves adapted to new needs have flourished in the 1970s. Victoria Deep Water Terminal at Blackwall opened in 1966 (above) handles cargo from Northern Europe, Poland, Portugal and the Mediterranean. The Freight Express-Seacon Terminal at Millwall (below) opened in 1976, since when it has handled an increasing tonnage of steel.

Photographs by Douglas Brown

was in future to be allocated to a regular employer and paid in accordance with the agreement in the port. This proposal was accepted and the P.L.A. found itself allocated 365 men from the T.U.R. The Aldington-Jones Committee recognised that this procedure was going to cause problems unless more men would accept voluntary severance and leave the industry. Over and above the existing severance scheme, therefore, it called for a special government-financed scheme to encourage unfit men and those over fifty-five to retire. Payments of up to £4,000 were offered during a period of six months ending in February 1973 and 2,458 men, 525 of them from the P.L.A. payroll, accepted the offer and left.

Before this procedure had been completed, another leading firm was in difficulties: Thames Stevedoring, a subsidiary of the giant Vestey Group, which employed 900 men. Here a very special problem arose for the P.L.A. The Vestey concern was deeply involved in the South American meat trade, which was important to the port. Hoping, in part, to safeguard this traffic, the Authority took over Thames Stevedoring, but it lost the meat trade, nineteen months later, to Southampton. Once this take-over had been negotiated, other decisions followed logically and almost inevitably. Independent operators in the port were clearly in such difficulties in the new environment that the P.L.A. felt obliged to take over stevedoring responsibilities itself. To create a viable organisation, the acquisition of Thames Stevedoring needed to be supplemented by other take-overs. The situation was thoroughly discussed with the unions and from these talks emerged the concept of a single employer in the port—the P.L.A. In April 1973 Metropolitan Terminals, employing 680 men at Tilbury, was taken over and in June 1974 Gee Stevedoring which employed 100 men in India and Millwall Docks.

The suspicion generated by the newly-emerging pattern of activity, particularly at new container terminals, led to a five weeks unofficial strike in the port early in 1975; its declared purpose was "to prevent the loss of jobs to registered dock workers". Almost certainly, this stoppage sealed the fate of Scruttons Maltby, which was the largest independent firm in the port, with 2,670 employees. Immediately the strike ended it approached the P.L.A. and within four months had been absorbed. To handle the work of all these organisations which it had taken under its wing, the Authority formed in 1975 a new company known as London Cargo Superintendents Limited, the name of which was later changed to Port Documentation Service Limited. With a staff of over 600, this organisation today provides a comprehensive and independent freight documentation service to shipowners.

At the time of writing, only one independent stevedoring firm is left in the Port of London: Wallis Smith Coggins, in India, Millwall and Tilbury Docks. The P.L.A. has become the largest stevedoring organisation in Europe, possibly in the world, and thus its responsibilities are greatly widened and the challenge facing it increased. Lord Aldington summed up in 1976: "We have to cease being principally an administrative authority with responsibilities for running the Port of London, and we have to become a first-class competitive commercial undertaking, offering the best port facilities and cargo-handling services."

The absorption into the P.L.A. of the men who had worked for the former independent stevedoring companies was marked by a new set of intractable problems. Pay, conditions and working arrangements had to be brought into line, and the two sets of men had to be integrated into a single labour force sharing the same skills. Their experience, however, had differed and a measure of re-training was necessary. A spirit of competition for jobs persisted, in a new environment in which co-operation was essential. As so often in this industry, the roots of conflict lay buried in history. Back in 1889, as we have seen in an earlier chapter, the old dock companies had conceded to shipowners a right to rent quays, sheds and cranes in some docks and to employ their own labour to discharge vessels. This "quay and shed space" agreement, for which some sort of case could be made in the days when a vast number of small packages had to be dumped on the quay to be sorted before they could be despatched or warehoused, had become unacceptable to the shipping companies. No such system operates in any other European port. Shipowners are ready to bear the cost of discharge as far as the ship's rail, and no further. Over nearly eighty years, however, the men who had been working the quay and shed space agreement had devised and applied their own protective, some would say restrictive, procedures, in established manning levels and in other ways. These so-called "ocean trade practices" they were very unwilling to change. In some cases, therefore, the unions insisted on maintaining quay and shed space agreements, though the P.L.A. declared that it was unable to sell such an agreement to a shipowner. There were occasions when to secure a cargo, the P.L.A. actually employed two sets of men for the same duties.

Lord Aldington, when he first became P.L.A. Chairman, remarked that "the extent of the changes now in full flow in the Port of London is almost frightening", and went on to comment: "At times of such change relations between employee and employer must come under strain, for simple human reasons. Many relations and practices and attitudes of mind rooted deep in history were, as it were, withered and blown away by the gale of change." There is no question but that in less than twenty years the whole aspect and character of the port was transformed.

The outside observer remarks a loss of movement and colour in the river scene and finds in the modern container berths none of the glamour attributed to earlier techniques of cargo handling. The port worker enjoys shorter hours, better pay, regular employment of a cleaner and less strenuous nature. But here we encounter a problem which has arisen in most industries as they have embraced new technologies: ancient skills often become irrelevant, and in those skills men have always taken pride, deriving satisfaction from their work even when it was harsh and hazardous. The lightermen well illustrate this point. One of the most remarkable books ever written about the Port of London was the autobiography of one of them, Dick Fagan. The lighterman, when fully trained, handled his immense dumb craft single-handed, using "sweeps" or oars almost thirty feet long. He had to cast off at exactly the right moment, to lug on the oars so as to take full advantage of the flooding water and to counteract any wind, to understand "the sets of the tide" in the different reaches of the river, to judge the time required to "drive" from one point to another, and to know how to bring his barge into a wharf smoothly and accurately. In this way, a lighterman could bring his cargo twelve miles in a single drive; there is one case recorded of a 16 miles drive, from Dartford Creek buoy in Long Reach to the Greenland entrance to the Surrey Commercial Docks. This was very hard work. A young apprentice's hands were

Lord Aldington, Chairman of the Port of London Authority, 1971-77. *Courtesy P.L.A.*

Jack Jones, C.H., General Secretary of the Transport and General Workers' Union, 1970-78. *Photograph by Peter Coppock*

often raw and his muscles strained after a difficult drive. Between the two world wars lightermen on occasion worked for twelve or fourteen hours at a stretch. Despite these conditions, there was a close fraternity and a fierce pride. Sons followed fathers and there was much inter-marriage of lightermen's families. And every fully-fledged lighterman was a Freeman of the River and a Member of the Company of Watermen. Two passages from Dick Fagan's book* suggest something of the attraction, as well as the skill and the danger, of the job:

"That shoot from Trig Buoy to Fennings Wharf had the reputation for being the nastiest of the lot for the following reasons. The buoy is situated just above Southwark Bridge on the north shore. Just below this bridge come the arches to Cannon Street station; just below that is London Bridge. It follows that once you leave Trig Buoy every second counts. There's no time to correct any margin of error. Because of the three bridges coming so close together the tide works up a terrific lick, the shoot through The Bridge into Fennings is with the fastest race of water on the Thames, and when you fetch up against the shipping at the wharf it's like trying to stop a mad horse in a matter of yards . . ."

"I like night driving. It had something about it that is hard to put into words. The river seems that much wider, you're alone in the darkness, almost alone in the world. You can think your own thoughts, if you have any, or you can sing and shout. Yours is the only sound in the surrounding silence. It's *your* river, *your* Thames, this is where you belong, this is home."

Not only the lighters, so much else has gone or is going. Most of the warehouses, with their fascinating variety of contents and the specialised skills they fostered. The stave yards, where coopers made and repaired the wooden casks which once took all the wine, sugar, tobacco, fish in brine, salt, fruit, vegetables and flour passing through this port. The coopers had been tightly organised ever since Henry VII in 1501 granted the first of several charters to the Coopers Guild. The P.L.A. ceased recruiting apprentices to this trade before 1930, but a few dozen coopers were still working in the London and West India Docks until almost 1970. The deal porters have disappeared, too. Until 1947 they stacked every piece of timber in the Surrey Commercial Docks, carrying the planks ashore on narrow runways with a "bouncing" stride which harmonised the body movement with the spring in the timber. They could run up forty or fifty feet high stacks of timber, and their colleagues measured and marked every plank. Then came the cranes, and later the unit loads of "packaged lumber". Even the dark-suited brigade in the port offices maintained an enormous pride in the port in the old days. "If you'd broken an old-type P.L.A. man in half, he'd have had the letters P.L.A. running right through him like a stick of Brighton rock," said one of them.

Men of the Tideway by Dick Fagan and Eric Burgess, Robert Hale 1966.

The Port of London and its workers struggled through a maelstrom in the 'sixties and early 'seventies into an entirely new ambience and atmosphere. Cruelly, it seemed, its great traditions actually counted against it. The advantages were with new ports, starting almost from scratch with new technology and newly-recruited labour. To help it through these difficulties, the P.L.A. had one advantage: a great deal of valuable property which had become surplus to its requirements. In 1970 there were 880 acres of dockland available for sale, an area almost as large as that of the City of London. The London property market was booming and the hard-pressed Authority saw a prospect of replenishing its funds. St Katharine Dock was sold to the Greater London Authority for £1.5 millions and at the same time negotiations began to sell the magnificent Trinity Square headquarters building, the St Katharine Dock House redevelopment (with the P.L.A. leasing back one floor as its new head office) the London and Surrey Commercial Docks, and the Cutler Street Warehouse. The sales continued through the 'seventies and raised well over £30 millions.

The land occupied by the docks which had closed offered the possibility of urban development on a unique scale: greater than anything that had arisen in London since the Great Fire of 1666, greater than anything possible in any other European capital. In 1971 the government set up a Dockland Study Committee to consider this opportunity. The P.L.A. favoured a balanced development which would provide new homes and leisure amenities, some office and commercial development, and a good deal of industrial development to provide new jobs for those displaced from the docks. The successful Continental ports had demonstrated the benefits of developing new industry close to port facilities. The P.L.A. also hoped to gain direct benefit from some of the development. In 1973 it took a 65 per cent interest in a new company, Riverside London Ltd., which was to plan and develop the old London Dock site. Planning permission was secured for a major office development on part of the land.

Unfortunately for the P.L.A., government policies delayed all development for years. On top of inflation and the collapse of the property market in the early 'seventies, legislation and projected legislation to limit gains from land sold for development delayed negotiations with local government authorities. For years the government pursued a policy of discouraging new development in London and the south-east of England, and gave financial incentives to firms to move to designated development areas in other parts of Britain. Not until 1976-7, with a change of emphasis in government policy, did specific dockland projects begin to move forward. By early 1978 two major developments were at last under way: Wapping Woodland, on the site of the old London Dock, which will provide homes for 5,000 people, several hundred new industrial and commercial jobs, and social and recreational facilities, and a housing scheme on the south side of the river, which, if plans mature, will eventually produce homes for 15,000, three large hotels and an American-inspired "merchandise mart" — a six million square feet trade centre which will be a shop-window for British manufactures.

Thus, in the late 'seventies, new hope burgeoned on the banks of the Thames and, despite the battering it had endured, a new confidence developed in the Port of London Authority and the other remaining port operators. If the painful lesson had at last been learnt that all whose future is tied to the port **must** pull together, there was a real chance that London could regain its position as a great, pace-setting enterprise. There was plentiful evidence of its capacity to succeed.

Tilbury is a fine modern port. Over £60 millions has been invested in the facilities on its 1,037 acres: 114 acres for container handling, 80 acres for forest products, 15 acres for the bulk grain terminal, five acres for RO/RO traffic, and plenty of land still available for further development. The biggest of modern bulk cargo ships can come into Tilbury. Cargo can be handled at ten times the rate of an old conventional break-bulk berth, with about one sixth of the labour force. It must be remembered, however, that revenue to the P.L.A. per ton of container cargo is only about one-seventh of that per ton of conventional cargo. By 1976, furthermore, the P.L.A. had not achieved a satisfactory return on its capital investment in the multi-user berths at Tilbury, despite the fact that they had been installed and paid for in or before 1970, when prices were significantly lower.

But the potential is there for performance matching that achieved anywhere else in the world, and frequently this has been achieved. Only a year after the container terminal for the Australian traffic had opened in 1970, it became the busiest container berth in Europe, with over 10,000 container liftings between ship and shore in a period of four weeks — a full 25 per cent above the target figure. Round-the-clock working on this and neighbouring berths has consistently shown high cargo through-put. From 1972 the four forest products berths handled over 1 million tonnes each year, except in 1975 (898,000 tonnes) and they achieved a record tonnage of 1.4 million in 1976. In 1971, too, one of the P.L.A. multi-user berths handled 750,000 tons of container cargo, including a regular container service to Leningrad which quickly developed into a trans-Siberian freight service to the Soviet Far Eastern port of Nahodka and so to Japan. Business built up steadily on the European Unit Routes and other lines to the Baltic, and a new West Africa Terminal was built and was operational in 1974. The Tilbury Rail Container Terminal opened in 1970, was handling one thousand containers a week by early 1971, and went on to a full 24 hours service in 1978. And, as described earlier, the Bulk Grain Terminal, on the riverside, was busy from 1969.

By 1977 Tilbury Docks were handling 294,500 containers a year — more than sufficient to place London at the top of the U.K. container-port league, and this figure excludes many thousands handled in the Upper Docks and on the private riverside wharves.

Improvements and additions to the equipment have come year by year. In addition to the Goliath and Paceco container cranes, and the massive straddle carriers, there are today forklift trucks which can lift four to six tons and swing the loads through ninety degrees, and at least one truck capable of lifting 40 tons. There are great banks of "reefer slots"—powered terminals into which refrigerated containers can be plugged. Containers themselves now come in many varieties: refrigerated and heated insulated boxes, tank containers for liquids and compressed gases, containers for bulk cargoes which can be discharged from them by gravity or under pressure. Though the length of standard containers can be as much as 40 feet, cargoes are measured in TEUs, twenty-feet equivalent units.

The most important recent development at Tilbury has been the construction of the Northfleet Hope Container Terminal, which began in 1976. The investment here was about £35 millions, of which £20 millions was found by the P.L.A. and the balance by two shipping organisations, Overseas Containers Limited and Associated Container Transportation Australia, ACTA, described as "the world's largest consortium of shipping lines". Northfleet Hope is a fully-integrated terminal covering about 64 acres, incorporating the earlier berth inside the modern Tilbury dock from which

Sir John Cuckney, appointed Chairman of the Port of London Authority in 1977, faced a financial crisis almost immediately. *Courtesy P.L.A.*

175

O.C.L. operated its Europe-Australia container service from 1970. A new, 1,000 feet-long berth was built on the riverside, on reclaimed land. The old and the new berths were designed to handle every week, between them, two or three of the largest container ships afloat. Thus they cover the requirements of the two shipping organisations serving Australia and New Zealand, including a large volume of highly specialised refrigerated cargo. Estimated through-put by the late 1970s is 170,000 to 190,000 TEUs a year. Apart from O.C.L. and ACTA, who continue to operate quite separately, other suitable users, such as Canadian Pacific vessels, have access to Northfleet Hope, which is managed by a new operating company called Tilbury Container Services, T.C.S.

And what of the Upper Docks: the Royals, the India and Millwall? The Royals were hard hit in the early 'seventies. The Jamaica Producers Steamship Company moved to another port the banana trade which since 1938 had brought a vessel every week to a specially mechanised berth in the Royal Albert Dock. Later the Australian and New Zealand meat trade, and then the Royal Mail, Blue Star and Houlder Brothers Lines to South America transferred elsewhere. By January 1972 ships ceased to berth along the north side of the Royal Victoria Dock. Considerable efforts were made to replace the lost trade. One shed was adapted to handle container groupage work, and this was steadily expanded so that by 1978 three sheds were busy in this way: a very successful adaptation to the different requirements of container transport. Three other sheds were developed for bonded and general warehousing of import cargoes; the level of activity and employment along the north side cannot compare with the days when it was fully operational for shipping, but the cargo stored in the quay-side transit sheds at any one time was greater by 1978 than when the berths had served the meat trade. In 1974 a new China Terminal was opened at the north-eastern end of the Royal Albert Dock to handle traffic flowing under a contract signed in Peking the previous year. Also in 1974 two new services to South America were gained, to replace in part those which had departed.

None of these successes, however, significantly affected a general pattern of decline in the Royals. By March 1978 only 14 berths remained operational in the whole of this mighty docks complex which only a couple of decades before presented a concentration of shipping such as might be seen in only two or three ports in the world. In 1977 the tonnage passing through the Royals was 960,000; that would have been a sizeable contribution to the trade of almost any other port, but it represented less than two per cent of London's total trade in that year (51 million tonnes) and it was only about a third of the 2.75 million tonnes handled by the Royals in 1970. As a postscript, however, it must be pointed out that the Australian and New Zealand meat trade lost to the Royals in 1973 came back to London in 1978 when the trade was containerised and directed through the Northfleet Hope Terminal at Tilbury.

In the India and Millwall Docks the picture has been more cheerful, and it is claimed that these today offer the most modern conventional dock facilities in the United Kingdom. Back in the 'sixties the first of a number of great new transit sheds went up, their curved aluminium roofs gleaming like the backs of silver whales. They may lack the architectural elegance of the original West India warehouses, but they are designed to meet the precise requirements of today. A pattern was set in 1967 when the "M" shed, now known as No 19 shed, in South West India Dock was opened with the claim that it was "one of the finest general cargo break-bulk sheds anywhere in the world". It cost over £1 million at that time, provided 163,000 square feet of space for transit cargo and 78,000 square feet more for warehousing, and was the first shed of its kind with an elevated roadway to give direct access to an upper floor. Nearby improvements were made to two other sheds to aid mechanical handling, and similarly at two sheds in the West India Export Dock. The Bulk Wine Terminal was transferred to the former Wood Wharf from London Dock in 1969, and in 1976 its storage capacity was doubled to two million gallons.

In the Millwall Dock the east quay is dominated by a modern development, the first part of which was built in 1966, with a major extension in 1970, to provide three large transit sheds on a 28-acre site. Here an express fruit service from the Canary Islands operated by the Fred Olsen Line discharges 2,000 pallets of fruit, about 1,400 tonnes, every week. It was the first operation of its kind in the world; 30 or 40 forklift trucks work on the quay and in the ship and discharge takes place through side ports. Near this activity, there is a groupage depot for containers, and on the opposite side of the dock there is another extensive and advanced cargo handling area around a vast building with a clear span of 150 feet.

Altogether there were 15 general cargo berths operational in the India and Millwall complex in 1977, as well as one timber terminal and a so-called "Combi" berth where containers carried by mixed conventional cargo/container-carrying vessels are handled. P and O use four nominated berths in West India and their contract provides just under half of the dock's total revenue. There are also important imports of fruit from New Zealand. Improvements to cost £400,000 were put in hand in 1977 and a new £600,000 heavy-lift crane was due for delivery in 1978. The number of men working in India and Millwall in 1978 was about 3,000.

The West India Import Dock, the most northerly of the three docks, has been phased out. In 1976 the south quay was "mothballed" and it was later announced that a scheme was being discussed between the P.L.A. and the Tower Hamlets Council to re-develop the north quay for light industry. On the site of the old "D" shed 32 separate industrial units were proposed and the old "E" shed alongside was designated as a possible new site for Billingsgate fish

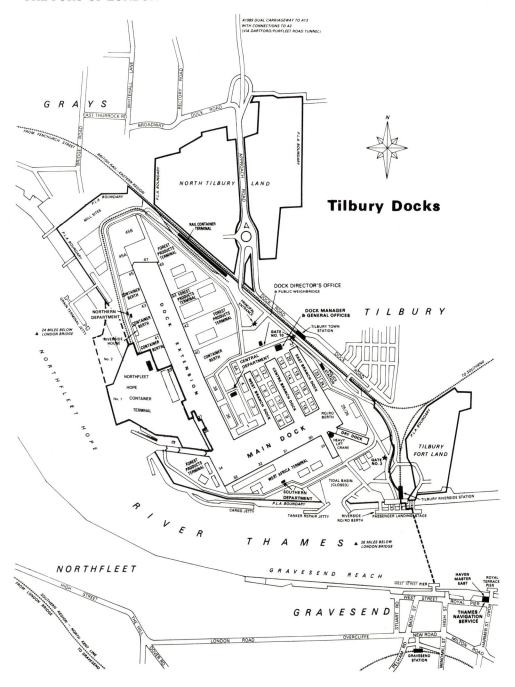

Tilbury Docks

Tilbury 1978. This map shows the layout of Tilbury Docks after completion of the Northfleet Hope Container Terminal in 1978.

Courtesy P.L.A.

market, which was expected to move from its ancient Thames Street site by about 1980.

Private wharfs on the river which survived the tough 1965-75 decade later picked up well. Purfleet Deep Wharf, for example, which handles a million tons a year of forest products and general cargo, opened a £2¼ millions extension in 1974. Alexander Bruce Ltd. at Grays is established as the U.K. terminal for the interesting "Seabee" barge service opened by the United States Lykes Line in 1972. Barges are carried on specially designed vessels, floated off when the parent ship comes to river moorings, and then towed to various berths in the port. Each barge is 97½ feet long and 35 feet wide and carries 833 tons, and since 1976 some of the barges have been built so that they can be dropped at sea and towed into port. The Lykes Line operates between Europe and the Gulf ports of New Orleans and Galveston. One of the most remarkable success stories has been that of Victoria Deep Water Container Terminal at Blackwall, opened in 1966, which is the only privately-owned common-user container terminal in the port. It started with only a score of men, but steadily built up business and work-force. By 1977 it dealt with approximately 450,000 tonnes of cargo carried on 470 vessels to or from Poland, northern Europe, Portugal and the Mediterranean—containers and unit loads. At a river-side wharf on the Isle of Dogs, just south of Millwall Docks, Freight Express Seacon Ltd have operated since 1976 a "London Steel Terminal" handling increasing steel tonnages through the port.

Many of the private wharves are equipped to handle forest products, with some specialising on newsprint. Several handle containers. A number have Customs facilities and several have their own rail links. Excluding the big oil companies' installations, a total of 36 wharves were listed in 1976 in the *Guide to the Riverside Wharves and Docks on the Thames* published by the London Riverside and Docks Trade Promotion Committee. Total trade at the private riverside wharves in 1977 was 9.4 million tonnes, excluding fuels and 5.3 million tonnes of aggregates—out of total cargoes through the port of 51 million tonnes.

London's recuperative powers have been amply demonstrated. But what opportunities are left to it as it faces a new decade? Many shipping lines today belong to the so-called "shipping conferences", which organise services on a regular basis, distribute cargo, agree on rates and pool revenue. These conferences account for about a quarter of world shipping, and for about a fifth of U.K. shipping. Most of the big shipping conferences have made the transition to container ships and have decided their European terminal ports. London's principal success has been the Northfleet Hope service. The last major conference decision came with the containerisation of the Europe-South Africa trade in 1978, and the U.K. port selected for that was Southampton. Shipping, however, is a highly competitive business and contracts are signed for fixed periods. A port which can provide a superior service or a more competitive price can always win traffic from a rival.

More traffic will be on offer in the years ahead. The National Ports Council forecast in 1977 a further decline in conventional cargoes until 1980 and beyond, with stability by about 1985. The decline was estimated to be from 12.7 million tonnes in 1975 to 8 million tonnes in 1985. But unit load traffic, it forecast, would increase from 27 million tonnes in 1975 to 53 million tonnes in 1985, and RO/RO traffic was expected to increase its share from 60 per cent to about two-thirds of the total.

This takes account, of course, of the increasing trade between the United Kingdom and Western Europe, a trend which began long before Britain joined the E.E.C. but which has accelerated rapidly. London, in the past, has failed to hold its share of this expanding trade. In 1971, when Britain exchanged 50.4 million tonnes with the E.E.C., 21.4 per cent of it went through London. By 1976, when the total was 64.5 million tonnes, only 10.5 per cent went through London. Approximately 80 per cent of this trade has been carried in containers and six out of every ten of these containers have travelled on RO/RO ferries. Felixstowe, Harwich and Dover have greatly benefitted.

London may have been ambivalent about RO/RO traffic because of a fear that it might easily become a subsidiary terminal feeding the great container ports of Rotterdam, Antwerp and Dunkirk. It has always been suspected that substantial amounts of deep-sea cargo destined for the U.K. have been unloaded on the Continent and then trans-shipped by RO/RO services. A specific case was monitored in 1974 when 50,000 tonnes of tea was discharged in Rotterdam and moved to Britain in this way. If this trend had developed, Britain's ability to handle oceanic traffic efficiently might have been threatened and the nation might have been at a disadvantage in maintaining its share of international trade.

In practice, as the container ships have come into service, the pattern has been established of calls at a number of European terminal ports. A theory advanced by the P.L.A. in 1967 has been proved: that there is important advantage in London's geographical situation in a "Golden Triangle" based upon Tilbury, Rotterdam and Antwerp, three ports which between them can serve efficiently the mighty urban and industrial complex of north-western Europe. The other two ports have long outstripped London in terms of tonnage handled, but they have not been able to undermine London's position as a world port.

The challenge facing London is to streamline its port facilities and its labour force to match a realistic assessment of future traffic, and to develop simultaneously services for oceanic and for continental shipping. The plan which the P.L.A. drafted, as long ago as 1968, for a new port built on the

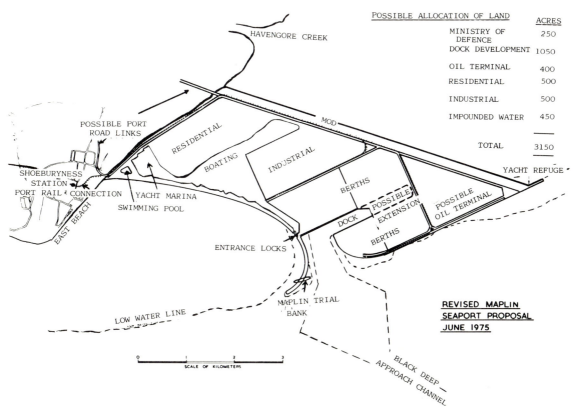

POSSIBLE ALLOCATION OF LAND

	ACRES
MINISTRY OF DEFENCE	250
DOCK DEVELOPMENT	1050
OIL TERMINAL	400
RESIDENTIAL	500
INDUSTRIAL	500
IMPOUNDED WATER	450
TOTAL	3150

Maplin. The proposals for a deep-water port at the mouth of the Thames were revised several times between 1968 and 1975 to take account of changes in government policy. This map shows the final plan, prepared after the decision not to incorporate an airport. *Courtesy P.L.A.*

Maplin Sands, off Foulness Island, offered a bold formula. The Authority spent almost £1 million on research and field studies, including boreholes, seismic surveys and siltation measurements. The plan was to recover 46 square miles from the sea by dredging and filling and to create an approach channel capable of receiving ships with up to 85 feet draught. That meant any vessel which could negotiate the English Channel. There were to be pipelines to the existing Thames oil refineries, and berths to take the largest bulk cargo and container ships. In 1969 the Thames Estuary Development Company was set up, a consortium in which the P.L.A.'s partners were big civil engineering and construction firms, the local authority principally interested, and a leading oil company. In 1972 the P.L.A. created a Maplin Directorate and in 1974 it submitted to the government detailed proposals for the seaport and an associated industrial development.

As the project unfolded, it became involved with discussion of London's need for a third airport and provision for this was built into the plan. When,

181

only two months after the P.L.A. completed its detailed proposals, the government resolved not to proceed with the airport, the whole Maplin project came to a stand-still. The dream has never faded, however. Options have been kept open and early in 1978 a P.L.A. spokesman said "Maplin is a good idea that will find its own time." Meanwhile, the big riverside terminal at Northfleet Hope was built instead.

It seems inevitable, at the time of writing, that the remaining upper docks — India, Millwall and the Royals group — must be closed before the Port of London has any real chance of being commercially viable again. Despite the deep emotions stirred whenever this possibility has been canvassed, such closures have been discussed for years. In 1973 a Docklands Study by the Department of the Environment and the Greater London Council accepted the premise that new technology would lead to the closure of the India and Millwall by 1978, of most of the Royal Victoria Dock by 1983, and of the remainder of the Royals by 1988. The P.L.A. was careful not to associate itself with these assumptions, but its spokesman admitted at the time that the future of India and Millwall had been looked at in the course of a normal review of P.L.A. resources relative to available trade.

In 1976 the P.L.A. announced a firm intention to transfer all general cargo activities from India and Millwall — mainly to the Royals — by the end of that year. It explained that the 14 berths still in use in India and Millwall Docks had been used to only 43 per cent of their capacity in the previous three months. A trade union-led campaign was quickly mounted to oppose closure, concentrating on the social effects in an area where there were already 12 per cent unemployed and where 30,000 jobs were estimated to have disappeared between 1966 and 1971. Critics of the P.L.A. argued that more vigorous marketing would produce more traffic. Some attacked the quality of P.L.A. management, some called for nationalisation, some blamed the government and urged it to inject money into the docks area.

In the autumn a Port Trade Development Committee was created, representing trade unions, local authorities, the P.L.A. and other employers, and shipping companies. Its chairman was Mr Frank Cousins, who had retired a little earlier from the leadership of the Transport and General Workers' Union. This Committee found there was little it could do to produce more traffic and its main finding was that the government should pay some of the cost of surplus manpower and should create an independent Industrial Development Board to seek other work for the docks and riverside communities.

At about the same time as this report appeared, the P.L.A. retreated from its proposal to close India and Millwall and instead announced concentration of traffic there in the Millwall section and at berths 17 to 25 in the South West India Dock. It promised to spend £400,000 on improving sheds and berths.

By May 1978 this change of attitude appeared to have been a mistake and, under a new Chairman and a new chief executive, discussion was renewed about the need to close *all* the upper docks. The P.L.A. annual report, published at that time, showed some improvement in traffic, but mounting losses. Total traffic rose from 45.6 million tonnes in 1975, to 48.6 million tonnes in 1976, to 51 million tonnes in 1977, and container traffic over the same period from 215 to 255 to 266 thousand TEUs. But the loss on day-to-day operations was £2.4 millions and, adding in "restructuring costs", the loss totalled nearly £8 millions. Reserves, which had stood at £54 millions at the end of 1974, were down to less than £2 millions. All the upper docks were shown to be loss-makers and projections for 1978 showed the losses likely to increase alarmingly.

The new Chairman, Sir John Cuckney, reported: "We are again reviewing the future of the upper docks, which are currently under-used, and forward forecasts of trade do not justify their retention for much longer." The P.L.A. published an information paper which declared bluntly: "From now on, if anyone requires us to keep open a dock that no longer pays for itself, they will have to pay us to do so. Otherwise it will close. And if anyone requires us to keep work-people whose work is not needed, they will have to pay us to do so. We can no longer pay them ourselves."

Again, the trade unions and the local authorities in dockland campaigned vigorously against closure. In July 1978 the Transport Secretary, Mr William Rodgers, vetoed the P.L.A. plan to close docks and asked the Authority to work out with the trade unions a programme for reducing manpower on the payroll and improving productivity. The Minister declared he would monitor improvements in performance and review the whole position at intervals and, meanwhile, the government would give up to £35 millions in grants to the port and underwrite a further £10 million of borrowing. Sir John Cuckney greeted this announcement with the assertion that it would "delay the re-establishment of a viable port" and he promised that the P.L.A. would in future publish separate accounts for the upper docks so that their drain on resources would be clear. The Royal group, he thought, might incur losses of £250,000 to £500,000 a month.

Looking back over the post-Devlin decade, one sees a Port of London in which men of goodwill proved unable to adapt their thinking and their behaviour rapidly or fundamentally enough to cope with the changes enforced by technological innovation, economic development and social advance. Most of those involved tried hard enough, and they had their successes. Some were tough, but their thinking was distorted by ancient emotions. Others were clear-sighted, but not tough enough. Frequent changes of government policy, and almost endless discussion of theories which might or might not have been applied, did not help. The P.L.A. was no blinkered, reactionary, free-enterprise employer, but a public trust authority obliged only to balance its books. From its creation, its Board included two trade union men, so that the organised labour movement had a voice in its planning and decision-making. Employment policies in the industry were in the hands of a Dock Labour Board with equal representation of employers and trade unions. The unions had the power which attaches to a long-established closed shop.

The Port of London provides an object lesson that the problems which assail British industry are not easily analysed and overcome, and that solutions must be founded on hard facts, whatever theories may be popular.

The challenge facing the Port of London can be met with hope. The P.L.A. information paper of May 1978 pointed out: "London still has many of the natural advantages that made it a great port in the first place. It has a benign estuary with plenty of land down-river for the new port facilities, with deep water and ample shore areas, required for the new patterns of shipping and trade. It is close to the major commercial areas of the Midlands and South-East—half of Britain's manufacture is within 100 miles—and to the ports and densely populated region of Northwest Europe. There will always be a port of some kind in the Thames. But whether in 20 years it will be the insignificant relic of long years of idleness, inertia and waste, or whether it will be a major port still based on Tilbury but with thriving terminals along the riverside, is largely up to us."

Northfleet Hope. The area of the latest riverside development at Tilbury can be seen in this aerial photograph.   *Courtesy P.L.A.*

CHAPTER TEN

The River Today

THE beauties of the river Thames are to be discovered in its upper reaches. From the Pool of London to the sea it has no scenic attraction, and very little architectural interest — except at Greenwich, where there is as perfect a grouping of classical buildings as can be found in Britain. On this site there was a royal palace for almost three centuries; Henry the Eighth spent much of his time there and it was the early home of his daughters Elizabeth and Mary. In 1694 Sir Christopher Wren was commissioned to design a new range of buildings as a hospital for seamen and the group as it stands today, known since 1873 as the Royal Naval College, is his inspiration, although completed by several other architects. Between the colonnades of the two main groups of buildings can be seen, from the river, the exquisite Palladian palace of the Queen's House, designed by another of England's greatest artists, Inigo Jones, and completed in 1635. High on the green, wooded hill behind is the Royal Observatory founded in 1675, through which runs the Greenwich Meridian. To appreciate Greenwich, it is necessary to go ashore, landing at the pier beside which the famous nineteenth century tea clipper *Cutty Sark* is now preserved in a concrete dry berth.

Those who wish to explore the Thames for pleasure can travel by boat during the summer months from Charing Cross Pier, where the whole panorama of Central London, embracing the Palace of Westminster, the modern cultural complex centred on the Festival Hall on the South Bank, and many other famous landmarks, can be viewed. Calling at Tower Pier, there is a glimpse of the dome of St Paul's in the background and a close view of the ancient walls of the Tower of London. Greenwich then provides a suitable climax for the trip.

Those who wish to explore the *port* need to sail from Tower Pier to Southend — a favourite steamer excursion for Londoners until 1966, when the daily service of Eagle Steamers was withdrawn. In 1978, however, a new river service was announced and London's status as one of the great tourist cities of the world should produce sufficient traffic to ensure a regular summer service. Before passing under the Gothic splendours of Tower Bridge, a glance up-river will take in the three low and slender arches of the New London Bridge, completed in 1973 near the site of that ancient bridge which was for

St Katharine transformed. The old St Katharine Dock is seen above during re-development as a yacht marina surrounded by the World Trade Centre (top left), the Tower Hotel (lower left) and new housing development (lower right).
Courtesy World Trade Centre

many centuries the heart of the port. Between London Bridge and Tower Bridge, the Upper Pool was still lined in 1978 with many once-famous wharves on either bank. There are no ships at them now, no cranes, no men, no activity. Until redevelopment takes place, they are a monument to the bustling trade of another age. Once through Tower Bridge, the modern development of St Katharine Dock on the north bank catches the eye. A new hotel is dominant, but behind and beside it the old dock basins have been transformed into an attractive marina where, beside the craft of present-day yachtsmen, there are a number of preserved vessels recalling the days of working sail on the Thames. Around the basins some of the old dock warehouses have been restored and modernised and given new uses as luxury flats, offices and chic boutiques.

A little downstream some of the old warehouses on the Wapping waterfront have disappeared and some have been converted to new purposes including bold conversions for residential use. There are also some large-scale municipal housing developments, including high-rise blocks. Where the old London Dock lay, there is a general impression of disuse and decay, an overall emptiness of purpose. On the opposite side of the river, there is similar desolation where the old Surrey Commercial Docks were once crowded with ships. Sailing down Limehouse Reach, the entrance to the old Greenland Dock can be easily identified, still with a glint of open water behind the lock, but that may soon disappear.

As the river loops the southern side of the Isle of Dogs, concentration should be on Greenwich, but there are two points of interest on the north bank: a painted sign on the river wall indicating the site of the Millwall shipyard where Brunel's great ship, the *Great Eastern*, was launched in 1859, and the neat, functional design of the new Seacon Steel Terminal. There are more high-rise flats and, on the opposite bank, a municipal housing development where once the Royal Navy Victualling Yard was situated and where, in 1513, Drake was knighted.

Beyond Greenwich the Thames turns northward and here, in Blackwall Reach, we are in what was once the busiest part of the river. A tug pulling a few lighters or a police or pleasure launch may be all the present visitor will see. The one remaining lock giving entrance to the India and Millwall Docks stands out boldly, a well-designed construction painted in blue with the P.L.A. insignia. Ahead the great Brunswick Power station, with tall twin chimneys, marks the site of the one-time Brunswick Hotel and Pier, where travellers in the East Indiamen spent their last moments before embarkation. Beside it the mouth of the river Lea is clearly identifiable.

Around another great bend the river flows into Bugsby Reach, where the Royal Docks complex lies directly ahead and a few ships may be glimpsed. The western entrance, however, has been closed and cannot

P & O Ferries operate a daily jetfoil service from St Katharine Pier to Zeebrugge. These craft skin the Thames at 50 mph. *Courtesy P & O Group*

easily be identified. Woolwich Reach lies parallel with the Royals' basins and still has a busy look, with wharves and jetties on both banks, a giant sugar refinery on the north bank where vessels of up to 20,000 tons discharge, and much new housing development on the south bank. Construction began in the middle 'seventies of a great Thames Barrage in Woolwich Reach; it is likely to be completed by the early 'eighties, by which time the cost may exceed £500 millions. This is the price of protecting London from serious flooding, which several times in this century has caused heavy damage to property. The Barrage will have ten large gates which can be raised or lowered to control the flow of water to the upper reaches and there will be four main navigation openings for shipping, each nearly 200 feet wide.

Further downstream, the empty shell of a once-great ship repairing yard makes a dismal sight, then there is the single remaining entrance to the Royals Docks, and then a tangle of metal and concrete which is Beckton Gasworks, the largest of its kind on the river. The river Roding enters the Thames at Barking Creek and immediately beyond it there is one of London's great sewage treatment works. There is a plan to create a landscape of greater attraction on the south bank, where until recently there was nothing but immense empty marshland. This has been reclaimed, there is a stark concrete river wall and, far back behind it, a few pale concrete buildings. They form the embryo of a new town, Thamesmead, where 60,000 people are expected eventually to live. A riverside promenade and a large yacht basin feature in the plans.

Now there is more evidence of industry, concentrated on the north bank: first, Barking Power Station, near which 470-feet pylons carry cables across the river to the southern counties; then Dagenham Dock, with the great Ford factory stretching back behind it. Fords acquired 500 acres here in 1925, reclaimed the marshes, and started building in 1929. The company's private jetty is half a mile long and is able to take vessels of more than 10,000 tons. It operates on a 24-hour basis, has full Customs cover, and handles a constant procession of ships and barges carrying completed cars and knocked down components for assembly overseas.

On either side of the river the land is very flat now, with few interesting physical features of any kind. In Erith Reach the north bank defines the boundary of the area where spoil dredged from the river is being constantly pumped to raise the level. On the south bank immense silos rise against the sky to house a recent Unilever development based upon the soya bean. Further along, the new Littlebrook power station has taken over from Barking as the biggest on the river; beside it, to store its fuel, are giant oil tanks. Long Reach contains numerous oil storage installations at Purfleet, on the Essex bank. Then, as Tilbury comes into sight, the south bank is crowded with large-scale industrial undertakings, principally cement manufacture and paper mills, with tall chimneys belching smoke.

The clean, pale outline of the Bulk Grain Terminal, with its tendril conveyor belts to mills nearby, marks the approach to Tilbury, but the Northfleet Hope development, although so important to the new Port of London, does not dominate the river scene. The whole concept is spare and severely functional; only when a container ship is berthed there and the great boxes move rapidly to and fro will the visitor be impressed. Much more striking is the old Tilbury Passenger Landing Stage, its wooden structure a pleasant ochre colour which glows in sunshine and creates a subtle suggestion of the excitement of travel beyond far seas. Most of the busy activity of the Tilbury Docks is beyond the lock and not easily seen from the river, but cranes and ships and great piles of containers stand out sharp against the sky.

Below Tilbury, and Gravesend on the opposite bank, the river widens and for the remainder of the way to the sea there are wide expanses of mud and sand at low tide, and endless marshes lying too low to be seen from a small vessel. Eventually, there is Sea Reach, the last, straight channel to the estuary and the North Sea. Its northern bank carries the big Thames oil refineries at Thames Haven and on Canvey Island: metal towers and gleaming globes, flares burning against the sky.

The river broadens, the land to the south recedes, Southend's mile-long pier cuts across the sands, there may be glimpses to the north of the Maplin Sands where dreams flourished and foundered; and then it is all water and the Thames has merged into the open sea, the sea across which the fleets have sailed for two thousand years, bringing wealth to Britain and taking the law and the lore of London to the whole world.

The nostalgic Thames traveller may gaze on the large crude oil tanker and dream of the carrack, or observe the container liner and yearn for the clipper, or watch the skimming jetfoil craft (which carries 200 passengers down the river at 50 miles an hour to Zeebrugge in 225 minutes) and wish for a paddle steamer. A river and a port such as this will always carry men's minds back to the past, because that past has been so colourful and so full of achievement. But the real men of the Port look to the future, and there they discern ample opportunities for further achievements which will write new episodes of drama into the history of London and its river.

Tilbury Passenger Landing Stage.

Photograph by Douglas Brown

190

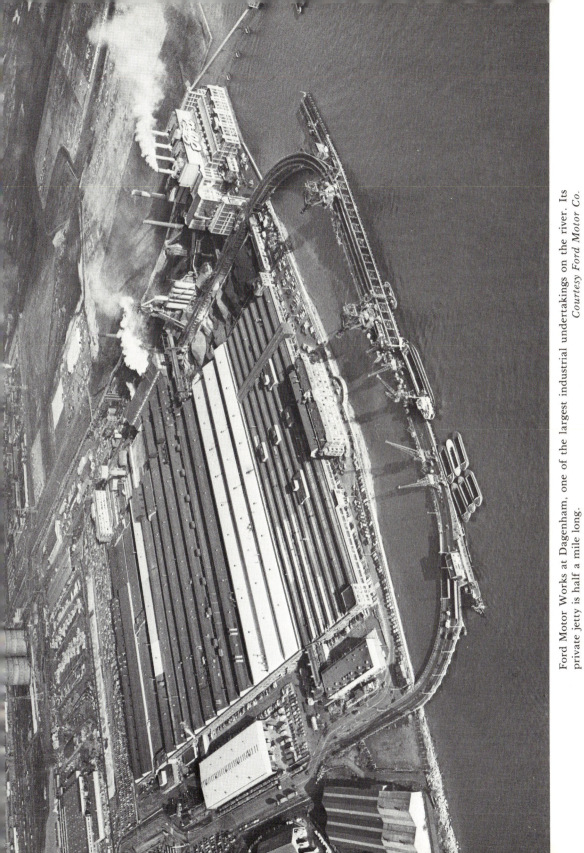

Ford Motor Works at Dagenham, one of the largest industrial undertakings on the river. Its private jetty is half a mile long.

Courtesy Ford Motor Co.

The Era of Dock Development

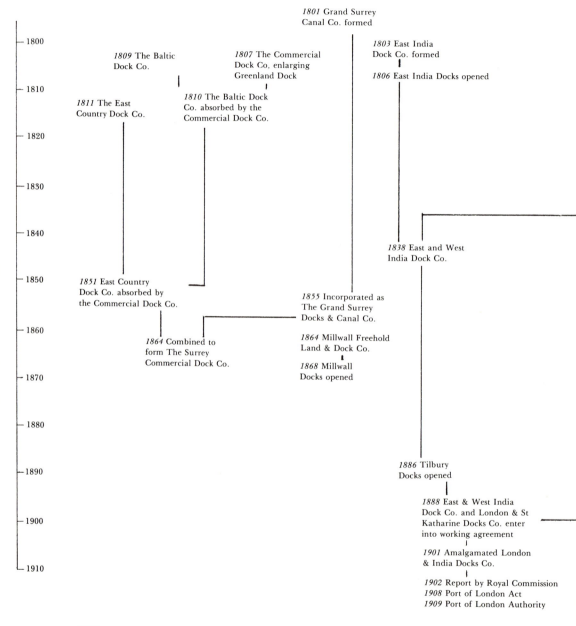

1801 Grand Surrey
Canal Co. formed

1803 East India
Dock Co. formed

1800

1809 The Baltic
Dock Co.

1807 The Commercial
Dock Co, enlarging
Greenland Dock

1806 East India Docks opened

1810

1811 The East
Country Dock Co.

1810 The Baltic Dock
Co. absorbed by the
Commercial Dock Co.

1820

1830

1840

1838 East and West
India Dock Co.

1850

1851 East Country
Dock Co. absorbed by
the Commercial Dock Co.

1855 Incorporated as
The Grand Surrey
Docks & Canal Co.

1860

1864 Combined to
form The Surrey
Commercial Dock Co.

1864 Millwall Freehold
Land & Dock Co.

1868 Millwall
Docks opened

1870

1880

1886 Tilbury
Docks opened

1890

1888 East & West India
Dock Co. and London & St
Katharine Docks Co. enter
into working agreement

1900

1901 Amalgamated London
& India Docks Co.

1902 Report by Royal Commission
1908 Port of London Act
1909 Port of London Authority

1910

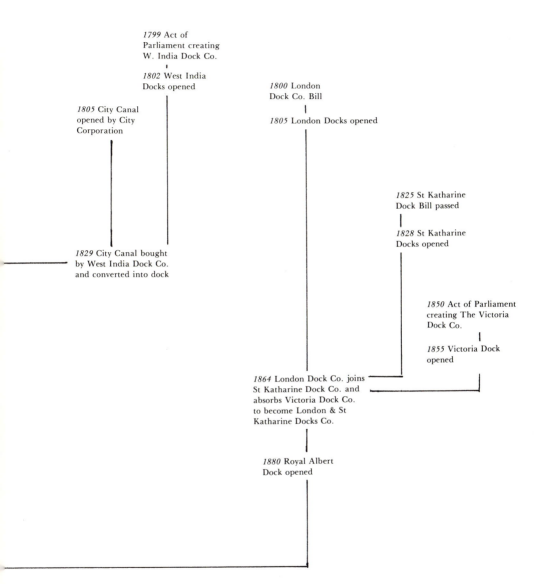

1799 Act of
Parliament creating
W. India Dock Co.

1802 West India
Docks opened

1800 London
Dock Co. Bill

1805 City Canal
opened by City
Corporation

1805 London Docks opened

1825 St Katharine
Dock Bill passed

1828 St Katharine
Docks opened

1829 City Canal bought
by West India Dock Co.
and converted into dock

1850 Act of Parliament
creating The Victoria
Dock Co.

1855 Victoria Dock
opened

1864 London Dock Co. joins
St Katharine Dock Co. and
absorbs Victoria Dock Co.
to become London & St
Katharine Docks Co.

1880 Royal Albert
Dock opened

APPENDIX II

Traffic Through the Port of London, 1700-1977

Year	Total Net Registered tons of shipping (millions)	Total foreign trade by value (£ millions)	Total foreign trade by tonnage (millions)
1700	0.652	10.263	NA
1750	1.160	13.956	NA
1795	2.714	31.442	NA
1851*	5.477	NA	NA
1909	38.511	322.614	NA
1920	32.759	NA	3.437
1930	58.086	603.743	NA
1939	62.086	NA	41.662
1950	50.249	NA	40.740
1960	89.191	2,750.000	57.143
1970	84.800	NA	60.420
1977	79.900	NA	51.000

*average of five years 1851-5.

APPENDIX III

Trade of the Port of London, 1970-1977

	1970	1971	1972	1973	1974	1975	1976	1977
Specialised facilities:								
Forest products ('000 tonnes)	985	971	1,078	1,226	1,208	898	1,283	1,20
Bulk grain terminal ('000 tonnes)	1,470	1,530	1,750	1,636	1,607	1,540	1,756	2,03
Containers ('000 TEU's)								
P.L.A. multi-user berths	NA*	232	269	183	178	141	169	18
Tenants' berths				89	97	74	86	8
Petroleum (million tonnes)	29.33	28.45	27.50	28.13	24.6	22.1	24.9	24.9
Coal (million tonnes)	8.42	6.53	3.98	4.56	3.6	4.1	2.8	2.9
Other goods:								
P.L.A. dock premises	NA	NA	NA	10.1	9.0	7.1	8.2	8.5
Other premises	NA	NA	NA	14.5	14.4	12.3	12.7	14.7
TOTAL TRADE (million tonnes)	60.42	57.42	54.00	57.24	51.5	45.6	48.6	51.0

*NA — Not Available.

Chairmen and Chief Executives of the
Port of London Authority, 1909-1978

Chairmen		*Chief Executives*	
1909-25	Viscount Devonport (Sir Hudson Ewbanke Kearley until 1917)	1909-13	Mr Robert Philipson
		1914-15	Mr Cumberland Lowndes
		1916-22	No C.E. but 4 Divisional Officers Chief Engineer, Secretary, new post of Dock and Warehouse Manager and Chief of Police
		1922-38	Sir David J. Owen (knighted Jan. 1931)
1925-41	Lord Ritchie of Dundee	1938-46	Sir Douglas Ritchie (knighted June 1941)
1941-46	Rt Hon Thomas Wiles	1946-48	Mr Theo Williams
1946-58	Viscount Waverley of Westdean (Rt Hon Sir John Anderson until 1952)	1948-64	Sir Leslie Ford (knighted 1956)
1958-71	Viscount Simon	1964-71	Mr Dudley Perkins
1971-77	Lord Aldington	1971-76	Mr John Lunch
1977-	Sir John Cuckney	1976-78	Mr William Bowey
		1978-	Mr John Presland

APPENDIX V

The Port of London

LIST OF PRINCIPAL TRADING AREAS SERVED

'000
Tonnes

10,164	Persian Gulf (mainly fuel imports)
3,143	Netherlands (two-thirds imports of fuels and basic materials)
3,009	West Africa (two-thirds fuel imports)
2,493	Mediterranean Ports (excluding Italy, Iberia) (70 per cent imports, mainly fuels)
1,933	Canada (mainly imports of foodstuffs, basic materials and manufactured goods)
1,927	U.S.A. (as for Canada but more exports of manufactured goods and petroleum)
1,115	Sweden (two-thirds import of basic materials and manufactured goods)
972	Australia (two-thirds imports foods, manufactured goods, fuels and basic materials)
939	France (two-thirds imports, mainly foodstuffs and fuels)
857	West Germany (two-thirds imports, mainly manufactured goods, some fuels)
837	Italy (seven-eighths imports, mainly fuels)
779	Central America and West Indies (over two-thirds imports, mainly foodstuffs and fuels)
603	South America (four-fifths imports, mainly fuels)
514	East Africa (mainly imports of foodstuffs)
498	U.S.S.R. (four-fifths imports of foodstuffs and fuels)
621	Belgium/Luxemburg (five-sixths imports mainly foodstuffs and fuels)
753	Finland (eight-tenths imports, mainly manufactured goods)
360	Far East Ports (excluding Malaysia) three-quarters imports mainly manufactured goods)
276	Spain
264	Denmark (mainly exports)
214	Poland (mainly imports)
213	Norway (mainly imports)
198	New Zealand (three-fifths imports)
194	South Africa
185	Malaysia
141	Irish Republic
120	India (two-thirds exports)
113	Portugal
70	East Germany

Source: NPC Annual Digest, 1976, Part II

196

A Selected Bibliography

The History of the Port of London, Sir Joseph Brookbank, Daniel O'Connor, 1921.

The Port of London, Yesterday and Today, D. J. Owen, Geoffrey Murray, 1927.

The Said Noble River, Alan Bell, P.L.A., 1937.

Liquid History, Sir Arthur Bryant, P.L.A. 1960.

The Port and Trade of London, Charles Capper, Smith, Elder & Company, 1862.

Guide for the use of visitors to the Docks and Warehouses, P.L.A. and Spottiswoode, 1913.

London's Riverside, Eric de Mare, Max Reinhardt, 1958.

London's Docks, John Pudney, Thames & Hudson, 1975.

Men of the Tideway, Dick Fagan and Eric Burgess, Robert Hale, 1966.

Stevedores and Dockers, J. C. Lovell, MacMillan, 1970.

The Dockers' Tragedy, R. B. Oram, Hutchinson, 1970.

Dockers, D. F. Wilson, Fontana, 1972.

The Docks after Devlin, M. Mellish, 1972.

The Dockers: Class and Tradition in London, Stephen Hill, Heinemann, 1976.

The Geography of London River, Ll. Rodwell Jones, Methuen, 1931.

London on the Thames, H. Ormsby, Sifton, Praed & Company, 1923.

The Library and the Picture Collection of the P.L.A., Bertram Stewart, The Richards Press, 1955.

Tracts by William Vaughan, 1793.

Government Publications:

    Report of the Royal Commission on the Port of London, 1902.

    Shaw Report on Transport Workers' Wages, 1920.

    Port Labour Inquiry, 1931.

    Essential Work (Dock Labour) Order, 1941.

    Dock Workers' (Regulation of Employment Order, 1947.

    Inquiry into the operation of the Dock Labour Scheme, 1956.

    Rochdale Inquiry into the Major Ports of Great Britain, 1962.

    Devlin Inquiry into Dock Labour Problems, 1965.

    The Reorganisation of the Ports, 1969.

    The Bristow Report, 1970.

P.L.A. Annual Reports, 1909-77.

Newspapers and Magazines:

    The P.L.A. Monthly.

    The Port of London.

    The Port.

    Polanews

Index

INDEX